CASABLANCA

CASABLANCA
SCRIPT AND LEGEND

Howard Koch

Preface by Howard Koch
Introductory Note by Ralph J. Gleason
Essays by Howard Koch and Richard Corliss
Reviews by Howard Barnes and Bosley Crowther
The Script by Julius J. Epstein,
Phillip G. Epstein and Howard Koch

THE OVERLOOK PRESS
Woodstock, New York

Manor

First published in 1973 by
THE OVERLOOK PRESS
Lewis Hollow Road
Woodstock, NY 12498

Library of Congress Catalog Card Number: 72-94412
First Printing 1973
Second Printing 1983

Grateful acknoweldgement is made to reprint the following material: "Introductory Note" by Ralph J. Gleason, Copyright © 1971 by Chronicle Publishing Company. "An Analysis of the Film" by Richard Corliss, Copyright © 1973 by Richard Corliss. Review of Casablanca by Bosley Crowther, Copyright © 1942 by The New York Times Company. Reprinted by permission. Review of Casablanca by Howard Barnes, Copyright © 1942 by The New York Tribune, Inc. Reprinted by Permission.

ACKNOWLEDGMENTS

As the "collector" of this multi-generational portrait entitled *Casablanca: Script and Legend* I wish to acknowledge the editorial assistance of Peter Mayer, Publisher of Avon Books and the Overlook Press, and my neighbor in Woodstock, New York. It was his idea to commemorate the thirtieth anniversary of *Casablanca* in this manner. I am also grateful to the various contributors mentioned in the table of contents along with Walter Bougere, whose interviews with students at Stanford University gave him a new insight into the film's significance for their generation.

TABLE OF CONTENTS

Howard Koch

PREFACE

At present anyone with an eight- or sixteen-millimeter camera can become a movie maker—whether for his family and friends (a captive audience) or, hopefully, for a wider circle and possible commercial distribution. Responding to the demand of today's youth, most of our universities and colleges have courses on the technique of film-making. It has become open season for the aspiring amateur armed with an idea and enough raw stock to put it on film—and the whole world is his shooting ground.

Yet only a few decades ago motion picture production was the private preserve of a select group of professionals entrenched in a Pacific enclave called Hollywood, where art and commerce met head-on and tried to reconcile their conflicts as best they could. Hollywood Boulevard was not exactly paved with gold, but underfoot are the copper-inscribed names of those who mined it in vast quantities during its lush period—along with more fame than is usually accorded princes and presidents. Reigned over by a half dozen tycoons in an uneasy alliance with labor bosses of the closed craft unions, it was not an easy world to penetrate.

For a writer there was then no prescribed way of preparing for a career in films, as there was in the other arts and professions. It was largely a matter of chance. Some succeeded by virtue of a Broadway hit or a best-selling novel; others entered by the back door through a relationship—son, nephew, mistress, or whatever—with a studio executive, star, or powerful agent. Or if you were an ex-

9

patriate Hungarian and adept at selling a story to a producer by acting it out over a cocktail at Romanoff's, you might pry your way in, at least temporarily, until they discovered there was less to the story than met the ear. Perhaps no writer entered the heavily guarded studio gates under stranger circumstances than I. In a figurative sense, I arrived from outer space.

For six months I had been writing the radio plays for Orson Welles and John Houseman, co-producers of the Mercury Theatre. One of the scripts turned some unfriendly Martians loose on an unsuspecting public with results that have become part of American folklore. The vibrations were felt in Hollywood. Orson moved his Mercury team to Paramount while I was offered a contract at Warners.

Since it was the Hollywood custom to type-cast their writers as well as their actors, I posed a dilemma for the studio. What do you do with a writer—a very junior writer—whose specialty was assumed to be Martians? Fortunately, this was before science-fiction became fashionable or I might have been writing about out-of-space monsters for the rest of my literary life. While the story department debated my future—or more likely just forgot about me—I waited in my office, trying to get used to the unaccustomed luxury of drawing a salary for doing nothing. Eventually, through the intercession of a friend, John Huston, a producer was induced to give me a chance to dramatize an historical romance starring Errol Flynn and entitled *The Sea Hawk*. The picture succeeded (i.e., made money) and I moved to a psychological drama, *The Letter*, with William Wyler directing and Bette Davis starring. And then came *Casablanca*.

Ralph J. Gleason

INTRODUCTORY NOTE

        The other night I dropped over to Rick's Place once more and found it had stood the years very well indeed.

"Rick's Place," for those of you who have been culturally deprived and are not familiar with one of the true romantic symbols of the World War II generation, more universally known I suspect than Harry's New York Bar, is the Café Americain in *Casablanca*.

And what I am talking about is the film *Casablanca*, with Ingrid Bergman, Humphrey Bogart, Dooley Wilson, and the rest. It was playing at the Telegraph Ave., Repertory Cinema and I couldn't resist such an excursion into pure, sweet nostalgia.

Casablanca was the film of my generation's youth, just as Bogart was the man and Ingrid Bergman the woman. Those were times when things were so much simpler; the good guys and the bad guys so much more clearly defined and the struggle itself, the moral imperative for man, so much more easily seen.

We had time for sentiment then. Was there a dry eye ever when Rick (interesting that over the years we remembered Bogart's name in the film was Rick but who remembered Bergman's was Ilsa?) gave the precious papers to Paul Henreid allowing him to take the lady and leave?

Casablanca summed up the morality of its time better, I think, than any other film ever has. Thirty years from now (*Casablanca* was set in North Africa in 1941) do you suppose that *Easy Rider* will look as good to today's young people grown then to middle age?

And Dooley Wilson, who played Sam, the black pianist and singer who made "As Time Goes By" into the nostalgic theme of lost love for all of us, made his debut in that film with a background version of "Shine" ("just because my hair is curly, just because my teeth are pearly"), which even today's racially hip audiences miss.

Everybody saw *Casablanca*. Everybody knew the story, knew the characters, and knew the context. When, three years later, a radio specialist in the Army Psychological Warfare branch wanted to let a friend in London know where he was, he started his letter from an APO address the way this column begins . . . "The other night I dropped over to Rick's Place . . ." and instantly his location was clear.

What a cast that was, too! Not only Bergman and Bogart as the lovers, but Peter Lorre, Sidney Greenstreet, and Claude Rains as the corrupt trio selling life to refugees in that terrible time after the fall of Paris.

And did any actor, including the great von Stroheim, ever play a Nazi officer with the precise arrogance and implicit evilness of Conrad Veidt? There were so many little touches: the Italian attaché and his eagerness to please; the resistance cadre headed by the character actor fresh out of *Ninotchka;* and the glorious German refugee waiter.

What made Bogart and Bergman so universal was their humanity, their vulnerability if you will. Bogart could afford to do a stupid thing, to be blind, and even to be supercilious. Bergman, well, all she had to do was to let those eyes fill with tears and the world was at her feet.

Surprisingly, the youthful Berkeley audience took *Casablanca* pretty much at face value. Now and then, especially in the scene where Bogart is sacrificing his own escape for Henreid and Bergman, the place was as quiet as a room full of living, breathing humans can be.

Now and then the sentimental parts provoked giggles or outright laughter, but it is hard, I suppose, to realize how sentiment can be real in another time and place. Delicate things like that are the first victims of changing times.

We could afford sentiment then, even in the darkest

12

days of Hitler's victories. Is there sentiment now in revolutionary circles, one wonders?

But *Casablanca* was back then, before all the words and all the images became distorted, drained of their truth by broken promises and failed ambitions.

Peter Lorre, of course, has just the right touch of rat-like energy and deviousness as he begs for respect, but for me, the secondary character who is without peer is Sidney Greenstreet.

As in *The Maltese Falcon,* Greenstreet's role could be played by no one else before or since. His size, that huge portly figure, is an asset, but it isn't just the size, it is the stance.

Sidney Greenstreet had the kind of presence that implied knowledge of all the rituals of affluence, intimacy with the practice of power, and a direct, analytical mind that saw the world (and acted in that vision) as being governed ultimately by the forces of evil implicit in man since Cain.

Having Greenstreet run one cafe, the Green Parrot (echoes of Sam Spade and the prior film) wherein the black market flourished and man was without honor even in misery, and Bogart run the other, where a kind of range rider mixture of compassion and amorality prevailed, was brilliant.

Bogart was the beautiful American expatriate, sportsman's honor, hard on the surface but sentimental inside. Loyal to his friends and above all to his employees, reserving judgments, capable of swift and violent action and of the quixotic gesture, the romantic self-sacrifice.

Casablanca was how we thought we were, all right, a pure explication of the mood in which we entered World War II and a greater distance than Mars even from the way we eventually came out of it, seduced by power, corrupted by affluence.

It was good to go back again in time to those days when, despite all our faults, we still believed in our own basic virtue. If today we are lost and by the wind grieved, it helps some to see us at a time when we were not, when the hope of truth and good and a positive affirma-

13

tion was not so far away as the grim reality of today makes them seem.

Casablanca was not very far in time or space from Spain and its spirit ranged on through the first few years that followed with the Maquis and the resistance until Algeria and Indochina and the rest brought down a backdrop of the kind of reality that makes the dreams harder to have any more.

The sentiment is rarer now and the whole visible world has a kind of institutionalized concrete dimness instead of the sparkle of life it had when Rick could let her go a second time, losing her forever in a cause that meant more than the lives of three little people in Casablanca.

14

Howard Koch

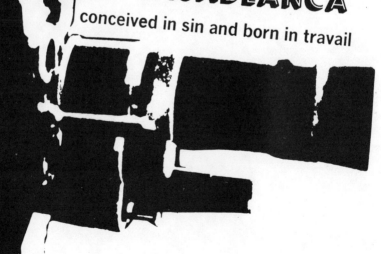

THE MAKING
OF CASABLANCA
conceived in sin and born in travail

As it approaches its third decade, *Casablanca* shows little sign of aging or diminishing popularity. Since its original release it has played more revival dates than any other film in motion picture history. Although it is not an art film in the usual sense, it is shown consistently year after year in art and university theatres over the country. More articles have been written about it than any other picture with the possible exception of *Citizen Kane*. At the University of Illinois it is the subject of a thesis for a master's degree. "Rick's place" was used as a military code for the city of Casablanca in World War II. Restaurants and nightclubs in many cities have been named for the film and one in Philadelphia has actually duplicated the set of Rick's "Café Americain." The title of the recent Broadway play by Woody Allen, *Play It Again, Sam,* needed no footnote to explain its origin. Everyone knew it was taken from *Casablanca* even though the actual words in the film were "Play it, Sam." No doubt the "again" simply underlined the average person's nostalgic memory of the scene (so familiar on posters and on the covers of film anthologies) in which Bogart sits drinking in the closed cafe while Dooley Wilson sings, "As Time Goes By."

Yet none of us involved in its production could have foretold that *Casablanca* was to have an illustrious future —or, in fact, any future at all. Conceived in sin and born in travail, it survived its precarious origin by some fortuitous combination of circumstances to become the hardiest of Hollywood perennials, as tough and durable as its anti-hero, Humphrey Bogart.

It all began when Warners purchased the rights to a play entitled *Everybody Goes to Rick's,* which fell by the wayside before it reached Broadway. The play provided an exotic locale (later to become newsworthy by reason of the Casablanca conference of Roosevelt and Churchill) and a character named Rick who ran a cafe where most of the action in the screen story takes place. In addition to Bogart the studio had a superb cast on call that included Paul Henreid, Claude Rains, Peter Lorre, Sidney Greenstreet, Dooley Wilson, and Conrad Veidt. However, Jack Warner and his production head, Hal Wallis, wanted a new face for the female lead instead of one of the familiar feminine stars on the studio roster. Their selection of Ingrid Bergman, a Swedish actress beginning her Hollywood career, turned out to be a felicitous choice. She possessed the personal qualities needed to portray the romantic idealist with conviction and without sentimentality and her slight accent lent authenticity to the character's middle-European background.

But at the time Miss Bergman was "owned" under the terms of a long contract by David Selznick and could only be pried away by the lure of a good story that would advance her career and her box-office value to the Selznick organization. Having nothing on paper to submit, Hal Wallis astutely dispatched Julius and Philip Epstein, two talented and fast-talking screenwriters, to Mr. Selznick, relying on them to improvise at least the semblance of an important story. They must have given quite a performance, because Selznick was sufficiently impressed to loan Miss Bergman.

But now the troubles really began. The Epsteins confessed to Wallis that the "story" with which they had entertained Mr. Selznick was actually a feat of verbal hocus-pocus without any real substance to provide a basis for a picture. Since the scheduled shooting date was only six weeks off, when the stars' costly salaries would begin, the news produced one of the crises so prevalent in Hollywood. The studio's method in such circumstances was to assign an additional writer or writers. I had just finished *The Letter*, so I was summoned to the front office and told to get to work on a film project entitled *Casablanca*, which had an imposing cast waiting in the wings and an accomplished director of action pictures, Michael Curtiz—in short, all the elements for a first-class production except the central ingredient, a story.

My collaboration with the Epstein brothers was enter-

18

taining and, to a degree, productive. They came up with all sorts of amusing lines and incidents for the various characters that were to people Rick's nightclub while I tried to fit the bits and pieces into a dramatic continuity, like working out a jigsaw puzzle. However, after a week or so we were unhappily aware that, while we had some interesting elements, they didn't add up to a workable story. It was as though we were building a house and we had some bricks and timber but no blueprints, no guide to the eventual structure. At this point we had to face the fact that our collaboration was not producing the desired result and time was pressing. Both the Epsteins and I were willing to bow out, more than willing, anxious to avoid what seemed like an impending disaster. The Epsteins, more experienced than I in the ways of Hollywood, acted with more dispatch. They asked to be transferred to another picture and the front office granted their request.

The morning I heard the news was not one of my happiest moments. I found myself holding a bag that, while not exactly empty, contained a miscellaneous jumble of characters, ideas for scenes, and atmospheric bits. In the movie world there is no substitute for success and no acceptable excuse for failure. The prospect was not promising.

In my anxiety to get something on paper, I tried all manner of approaches. Should we begin the picture in Paris where Rick (Bogart) and Ilsa (Bergman) met and fell in love and then lost each other when the Germans marched into the city? . . . No, that would explain too much about Rick when we meet him as a cafe proprietor in Casablanca. Better to keep his background a mystery to be revealed bit by bit as the story progresses. Rick should be an enigma that intrigues the French prefect, Louis Renault, to be played by Claude Rains. The ambiguous, cat-and-mouse relationship of the two men, each with a wary respect for the other, eventually became the thread which wound its way through the story and held it together, although at the time I hadn't the faintest idea where it was leading.

With the deadline creeping up on me and with Mike Curtiz asking when was he going to get pages, a kind of

19

paralysis came over me. I remember sitting in my corner office of the writers' building, staring out the window at the yellow-blooming acacia trees for one whole day. There was a mockingbird in the tree and, if you've got a mockingbird, you don't need any other because he has the whole repertoire of bird songs. This one had even added the flirtatious whistle that he'd probably picked up from some sailor on the make for a pretty girl. Or was the bird mocking me for wasting a precious day as though I expected a story to fly in through the open window?

Finally, in desperation, I decided to forget there was no story line and just start writing scenes as they came to me and using the Epstein material wherever it fitted in. I had only the vaguest notion where each scene was leading, just hoping that it would lead to another scene and another and that the sum total, if I lived that long, would add up to a film that wouldn't be bad enough to end my brief career in Hollywood.

On my desk, sharpened by my patient secretary, were a dozen brown pencils, Eagle Number One. I'd learned to have great respect for these pencils and use them to this day. Sometimes they seemed to take off on their own with me merely holding them, like the marker on a ouija board. The pencil obediently wrote down the two words that open every screen play—*Fade In.*

But fade in on what? Obviously the first thing was to establish the atmosphere. Fortunately, the Epsteins had done their research well and had bequeathed me some lively and often humorous incidents that graphically evoked the time and place. Casablanca was Moslem and during the Second World War it was a way station for refugees fleeing from German-occupied Europe to neutral countries. And it was notoriously corrupt. There was little distinction between the Vichy authorities who were supposed to enforce the laws and the criminals who made a living by breaking them. They were two sides of the same coin and often worked profitably together. As in Saigon of the sixties, anything could be bought and sold on the black market—foreign currency, jewels, visas, girls, even human lives.

Once the atmosphere is established, the story must be-

20

gin to move. I went through the rich assembly of actors waiting to take their parts in the story and picked Peter Lorre (Ugarte) as the one to initiate the action. With his round baby face and wide, bulging eyes Peter could mask his deviousness under a self-mocking innocence. Like his partner in crime, Ferrari, played by Sidney Greenstreet, he is a natural to be involved in black-market operations. In his opening scene we learn that he has acquired two letters of transit signed by General Weygand, granting the bearer the right to travel without passport or visa. He entrusts them to Rick for safekeeping until he can dispose of them at a fancy price. But two German couriers have been killed and we suspect that Ugarte has engineered their murder to gain possession of the valuable letters. A high Nazi official, Strasser, played by Conrad Veidt, has arrived in Casablanca accompanied by several subordinates. To impress the Germans, whom he secretly despises, Renault makes a big show of arresting Ugarte in their presence while dining in Rick's cafe. Ugarte, trying to escape, shoots at one of the police but is overpowered and presumably taken out to be executed.

As I come to this scene, I remind myself to play down the melodrama, letting the incident cause a minimum of commotion in the cafe—to give the impression that violence is endemic to wartime Casablanca. As after a shower quickly over and forgotten, the music and dancing resume and life goes on at Rick's as though nothing had happened.

The next question presents itself and the answer should open up new possibilities. Why has a Nazi official as important as Strasser come to Casablanca? Not just to insure the arrest of the man who killed the German couriers. He must obviously be after bigger game. Now is the time to plant the expected arrival of Strasser's antagonist —a man we must project as the crusading leader of Europe's anti-Nazis, by name Victor Laszlo and to be played by Paul Henreid. After escaping from a concentration camp, he has so far succeeded in eluding capture by the Germans. Although Casablanca is nominally unoccupied territory, the Germans control it through their

Vichy stooges and Strasser warns Renault that Laszlo must never leave Casablanca, at least not alive.

Rick is our lead. Where does he stand at this point? Although Strasser's dossier reveals that Rick fought for the Loyalists during the fascist invasion of Spain, he professes no interest in politics. In the Ugarte incident he took a neutral position and, when questioned by Renault, he dismisses the subject: "I stick my neck out for nobody."

But by now we have also planted a woman with Laszlo, presumably his wife or mistress. And stories being what they are, the woman will be, of course, Ilsa (Ingrid Bergman), with whom Rick had the romantic affair in Paris.

Two weeks away from the scheduled shooting date, I recall taking stock of where we were (the "we" including the Epsteins, whose material I used in the sequence along with my own). Numerically, we had about forty pages, a quarter of the eventual screenplay. They were typed and sent to Curtiz, who quickly responded with enthusiasm, although I think Mike was so worried and hungry for a script that any pages would have looked good to him. The forty pages were mimeographed and sent to the various departments—casting, camera, set construction, montage, location, music, and special effects—that were assigned to the production.

From a story standpoint what did we have working for us at this juncture? In broad melodrama terms, we had established the bad guys (the Germans) and the good guy (Laszlo) and in an equivocal position between these extremes were Rick and Renault, both professedly cynical and out only for themselves. We also had a tangible stake —the letters of transit that had accidentally fallen into Rick's hands. I made a mental note that these could be useful later as the object of contention (how useful I didn't realize at the time). The dramatic question at the heart of the picture was beginning to emerge. How would Rick act in a crisis when confronted with an unavoidable choice between taking one side or the other or, to put it another way, between his own interests and his real

22

sympathies? Complicating that choice was a woman who had loved him and left him to share with Laszlo his life and his political mission.

The structure of the film was at last taking shape. In a general way I knew where we were going but I was also aware that we had a long way to go before Rick made his ultimate decision and the story was resolved. In the intervening section situations had to be developed involving the various characters and building toward the climax and denouement. I still had Epstein material but it was not in any continuity. Again I picked up my pencil and hoped somehow it would find its way through the intricacies of the evolving plot. The story, as it finally emerged, is in the text that follows and the text is in almost every detail the picture as it appears on the screen.

Reading it at this distance, the story seems to proceed naturally from its dramatic premise and the conflicting interests of the characters. But at the time all I could see ahead of me were a hundred blank pages with forty or so people—director, actors, technicians—waiting impatiently for each scene when (and if) it came into existence.

Fortunately, I had the help and encouragement of Humphrey Bogart and the other principals in the cast who had become aware that we were in a Pirandello situation—six characters in search of a story. Bogey would invite me into his dressing-room with his usual "relax and have a drink." We would talk and sometimes a genie popped out of the whiskey bottle and off I'd go to develop the idea into a scene.

By the day shooting commenced, I had roughly the first half completed—about 65 pages of script—and to my astonishment, it seemed to be building, creating its own tensions. But a vast unknown territory lay ahead with only signposts here and there to guide me. The race was on between my pencil and the camera. I began to think of the camera as a monster devouring my pages faster than I could write them. About two-thirds of the way through the production, it was a dead heat. I was getting the scenes down to the set on the morning they were to be shot. I received a memo reminding me that any day on which the cast had no material to shoot would cost the studio thirty thousand dollars. This warning didn't add to my peace of mind.

At the same time a new complication developed. During the initial stages, Curtiz, worried by the absence of a script, was so relieved to see pages accumulating that he accepted them without reservation or with slight modifications that were usually constructive. However, as the screenplay began to take its final shape, Mike was assailed by second thoughts and doubts. Accustomed to success on a certain level, he dreaded the possibility of a box-office failure.

In this uncertain state of mind he did what was so often the practice of producers and directors. He started giving out the incomplete script to various colleagues on the lot for their opinions. Inevitably, the reactions varied and Mike's attitude toward the emerging story shifted with the changing winds. I only discovered what was happening when revised pages came through from the stenographic department with changes I knew nothing about. Obviously Mike was scavenging ideas from sources unknown to me. When I protested that some of the changes were illogical and out of character, he would answer impatiently in his Hungarian idiom, "Don't worry what's logical. I make it go so fast no one notices."

As the distance between script and shooting narrowed and the pressures increased, our disagreements erupted into quarrels. I felt as though I were trying to design a solid structure while others were changing the blueprint in the course of construction. Mike, on his part, contended his directorial prerogatives were being challenged by a writer—and a writer not too well established at that.

From my present perspective I can be more objective. I realize the difference between us was mostly a matter of emphasis. Mike leaned strongly on the romantic elements of the story while I was more interested in the characterizations and the political intrigues with their relevance to the world struggle against fascism. Surprisingly, these disparate approaches somehow meshed and perhaps it was partly this tug-of-war between Curtiz and me that gave the film a certain balance.

One disagreement I remember arose over the flashback

24

sequence in which Rick recalls his Paris love affair with Ilsa. I argued that these could only be conventional scenes with no dramatic progression until the end shot when Ilsa fails to show up at the railroad station. While they illustrated the cause of Rick's bitterness and cynicism, I felt these were sufficiently exposed in the cafe scene with Ilsa. And I was afraid that the flashback would dissipate the tension that was building in the present.

However, in retrospect I suspect Mike was right. Probably at this point the romantic interlude was a useful retard and relief from tension—and the viewer needed some visual proof of the ardor of the love affair to be convinced of its profound effect on Rick. At any rate, Mike exercised his directorial prerogative and the sequence was written and shot in accordance with his ideas.

The final weeks were a nightmare of which I remember only fragments. When I sent down to the set the last scene and wrote *The End* on the screenplay, I felt like a weary traveler who had arrived at a destination but with only the foggiest notion where he was or how he had got there. In January, 1943, when the picture opened at Warner's Hollywood Theatre, I wondered what all the excitement was about. I was still blind to the virtues of the film and saw only what I considered its faults. When a year later it received the Academy Award, I was by that time inured to miracles.

In the course of the years many films have won Academy Awards. Also we can admit, without excess modesty, that there have been more profound films than *Casablanca*. On close examination we can find a number of inconsistencies and illogicalities. (I should know!) Judged as a realistic picture of political events in North Africa, it would fall far short of a film like *The Battle of Algiers*. Moreover, in these days when each action movie, whether western or war or crime, tries to outdo its predecessor in brutality and blood-letting, *Casablanca* is curiously lacking in overt violence. In only three scenes is there any gunplay and these are brief and understated. Most of the tension derives from dangers implicit in the situations and atmosphere and much of the conflict is in the realm of ideas. It would seem that the film retains its popularity not because it conforms to the contemporary mood but in spite of it. What then is there about *Casablanca* that it continues to inspire the affection and loyalty of so many people?

There are almost as many reasons given for its durability as there are critics, columnists, and miscellaneous movie buffs who have tried to analyze it. Richard Corliss, editor of the magazine *Film Comment,* has offered his analysis in a later section of this book. He has discovered overtones and reverberations in the film of which I, at least, was not conscious. Perhaps the important function of a critic is to reveal to an author—and to the public—what he himself can neither analyze nor articulate.

Among the young generation a sort of mystique has grown up around the film and its protagonist, Bogart. Students tell me of "Casablanca Clubs" in some colleges whose members are expected to attend a showing each time it is revived in their area. Some have reported seeing it as many as fifteen times. When I took part in a student seminar on films at Stanford University, I asked why this impassioned loyalty to a movie made over a quarter of a century ago. One of the students, Walter Bougere, volunteered to interview young people in the Stanford community in some depth to find their answers to my question.

Reading their comments, I was struck by their consistency. Different words but the same trend of thought and feeling about the film and its significance to them, indicating to me that they were speaking for a large cross-section of young people. And their candid reactions taught me not only more about *Casablanca* but more about themselves and the counter-culture than I've gathered from all the television panels and articles by their elders. Perhaps in reacting to a fictional world, those students could more easily expose their feelings about the real world as they find it today—and the world as it might be if evil didn't parade as good and if right and wrong could be as clearly defined in our society as in their individual consciences—and as it is in *Casablanca.*

I was moved by their comments because they reveal a

26

latent idealism under the protective mask of cynicism—
like the tough-tender stance of Bogart's Rick in the film.
However, the times and the political circumstances are as
different as World War II was from Vietnam. In the end
Rick found an outlet for *his* repressed idealism, something
worth a personal commitment and sacrifice. And they
can't—or at least they haven't up to now—and our world
is the worse for providing no comparable moral alternative.

As I look back at the film's chaotic genesis, I share
some of their mysticism and nostalgia. I like to think it
achieved its real identity by some affinity with this new,
searching generation and, no matter who owns it in a legal
sense, *Casablanca* now belongs to its youthful fans.

Warner Bros. Pictures, Inc.
presents

CASABLANCA

HUMPHREY BOGART
INGRID BERGMAN
PAUL HENREID
CLAUDE RAINS
CONRAD VEIDT
SYDNEY GREENSTREET
PETER LORRE
S. Z. SAKALL
MADELEINE LeBEAU
DOOLEY WILSON
JOY PAGE
JOHN QUALEN
LEONID KINSKEY
CURT BOIS

Producer   Hal B. Wallis
Director   Michael Curtiz
Play   Murray Burnett, Joan Alison
Screenplay   Julius J. Epstein, Philip G.
Epstein, Howard Koch
Photography   Arthur Edeson
Film Editor   Owen Marks
Sound   Francis J. Scheid
Art Director   Carl Jules Weyl
Makeup   Perc Westmore
Set Decorations   George James Hopkins
Gowns   Orry-Kelly
Music   MAX STEINER

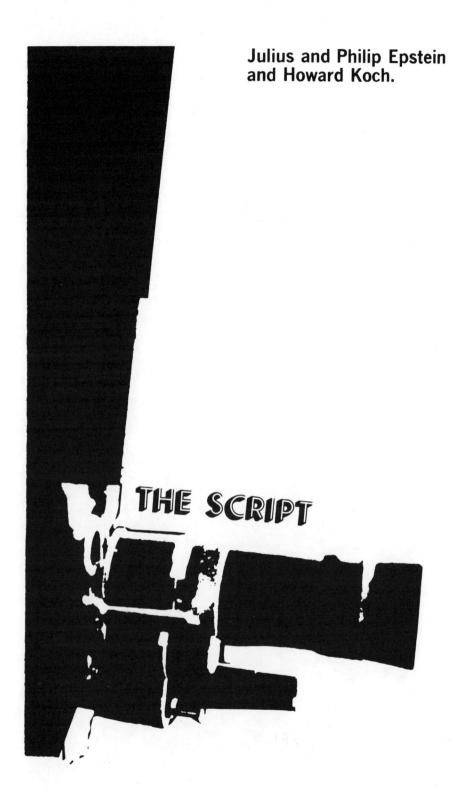

Julius and Philip Epstein
and Howard Koch.

THE SCRIPT

A long shot of a revolving globe. As it revolves, lines of fleeing refugees are superimposed over it. Over this scene comes the voice of a narrator.

Narrator
With the coming of the Second World War, many eyes in imprisoned Europe turned hopefully, or desperately, toward the freedom of the Americas. Lisbon became the great embarkation point. But not everybody could get to Lisbon directly; and so, a tortuous, roundabout refugee trail sprang up.

An animated map illustrates the trail as the narrator mentions the points.

Narrator
Paris to Marseilles, across the Mediterranean to Oran, then by train, or auto, or foot, across the rim of Africa to Casablanca in French Morocco. Here, the fortunate ones through money, or influence, or luck, might obtain exit visas and scurry to Lisbon, and from Lisbon to the New World. But the others wait in Casablanca, and wait, and wait, and wait.

A full shot of the old Moorish section of the city at daytime. At first only the turrets and rooftops are visible against a torrid sky. The camera pans down the facades of the Moorish buildings to a narrow, twisting street crowded with the polyglot life of a native quarter. The intense desert sun holds the scene in a torpid tranquility. Activity is unhurried. The narrator's voice fades away.

A police officer takes a paper from the typewriter. He turns to a microphone and reads.

Officer
To all officers! Two German couriers carrying important official documents murdered on train from Oran. Murderer and possible accomplices headed for Casablanca. Round up all suspicious characters and search them for stolen documents. Important!

31

A street in the old Moorish section. An officer blows his whistle several times. Native guards are rounding up people. Others are trying to escape. There is pandemonium. A police car full of officers screams through the street and stops in the market.

At a street corner two other policemen have stopped a white civilian and are talking to him.

1st Policeman
May we see your papers?

Civilian
nervously
I don't think I have them on me.

1st Policeman
In that case, we'll have to ask you to come along.

Civilian
patting his pockets
Wait. It's just possible that I . . .
Yes, here they are.

He brings out his papers. The 2nd policeman examines them.

2nd Policeman
These papers expired three weeks ago. You'll have to come along.

Suddenly the civilian breaks away and starts to run wildly down the street. The policeman shouts "Halt!," but the civilian keeps going, at one point passing Jan and Annina Brandel, a refugee Bulgarian couple. A shot rings out, and the man falls under a large poster of Marshal Petain which reads: "Je tiens mes promesses, même celles des autres." The policemen frantically search the body merely to find Free France literature against the Vichy government.

An inscription, "Liberté, Egalité, Fraternité," is carved
32

in a marble block along the roofline of a building. The camera pans down the facade, French in architecture, to the high-vaulted entrance over which is inscribed, "Palais de Justice." The camera continues to pan down to the entrance, where the arrested suspects are being led in by the police.

A sidewalk cafe on one side of the square. A middle-aged English couple are sitting at a table observing the commotion in front of the prefecture. A dark-visaged European, sitting at a table nearby, is watching the English couple more closely than the scene on the street.

Englishwoman
What on earth's going on there?

Englishman
I don't know, my dear.

Dark European
Pardon, pardon, M'sieur, pardon Madame, have you not heard?

Englishman
We hear very little, and we understand even less.

Dark European
Two German couriers were found murdered in the desert.
with an ironic smile
The unoccupied desert. This is the customary roundup of refugees, liberals, and uh, of course, a beautiful young girl for M'sieur Renault, the Prefect of Police.

Across the street, in front of the Palais de Justice, refugees are unloaded from the police van.

Dark European
Unfortunately, along with these unhappy refugees the scum of Europe has gravitated to Casablanca. Some of them have been waiting years for a visa.
puts his arms compassionately around the Englishman

33

I beg of you, M'sieur, watch yourself. Be on guard. This place is full of vultures, vultures everywhere, everywhere.

Englishman
a little taken aback by this sudden display of concern
Ha, ha, thank you, thank you very much.

Dark European
Not at all. Au revoir, M'sieur. Au revoir, Madame.

He leaves. The Englishman, still a trifle disconcerted by the European's action, looks after him.

Englishman
Au revoir. Amusing little fellow, what? Waiter!

As he pats his breast pocket there is something lacking.

Englishman
Oh. How silly of me.

Englishwoman
What, dear?

Englishman
I've left my wallet in the hotel.

Englishwoman
Oh.

Suddenly he looks off in the direction of the departed dark European, the clouds of suspicion gathering. But now, overhead, the drone of a low-flying airplane is heard. Heads look up.

A shot of an airplane overhead, its motor cut for landing. The refugees waiting outside the Palais de Justice follow the flight of the plane. In their faces is revealed one hope they all have in common, and the plane is the symbol of that hope.

Jan and Annina are looking up at the plane.

Annina
wistfully
Perhaps tomorrow we'll be on that plane.

Near the airport, the plane is swooping down past a neon sign on a building at the edge of the airport. The sign reads, "Rick's Café Americain."

As the plane lands, a swastika on its tail becomes visible.

The plane taxis to a group of people at the terminal. As it comes to a stop, soldiers march into a formation in front of it. In the group waiting is Captain Louis Renault, a French officer appointed by Vichy as Prefect of Police in Casablanca. He is a handsome, middle-aged Frenchman, debonair and gay, but withal a shrewd and alert official. With him are Herr Heinze, the German consul, Captain Tonelli, an Italian officer, and Lieutenant Casselle, Renault's aide.

When the plane door is opened, the first passenger to step out is a tall, pale German with a smile that seems more the result of a frozen face muscle than a cheerful disposition. On any occasion when Major Strasser is crossed, his expression hardens into iron. Herr Heinze steps up to him with upraised arms.

Heinze
Heil Hitler.

Strasser
with a more relaxed gesture
Heil Hitler.

They shake hands.

Heinze
It is very good to see you again, Major Strasser.

Strasser
Thank you. Thank you.

Heinze takes Strasser over to Renault.

Heinze
May I present Captain Renault, Police Prefect of Casablanca. Major Strasser.

The two shake hands.

Renault
courteously, but with just a suggestion of mockery beneath his words
Unoccupied France welcomes you to Casablanca.

Strasser
in perfect English, smiling
Thank you, Captain. It's very good to be here.

Renault
Major Strasser, my aide, Lieutenant Casselle.

As they acknowledge each other, Captain Tonelli barges in front of Casselle and salutes Strasser.

Tonelli
Captain Tonelli, the Italian service, at your command, Major.

Strasser
That is kind of you.

Renault leads Strasser toward the edge of the airfield, where their cars await them. Heinze follows, with Casselle and Tonelli bringing up the rear, engaged in a heated exchange of words.

Renault
again the suggestion of a double-edged implication
36

You may find the climate of Casablanca a trifle warm,
Major.

Strasser
Oh, we Germans must get used to all climates, from Russia
to the Sahara.
with a slight smile
But perhaps you were not referring to the weather.

Renault
sidesteps the implication with a smile
What else, my dear Major?

Strasser
casually
By the way, the murder of the couriers, what has been
done?

Renault
Realizing the importance of the case, my men are rounding
up twice the usual number of suspects.

Heinze
We already know who the murderer is.

Strasser
Good. Is he in custody?

Renault
Oh, there is no hurry. Tonight he'll be at Rick's. Everybody comes to Rick's.

Strasser
I have already heard about this cafe, and also about Mr.
Rick himself.

*Outside the entrance to Rick's, people are arriving. From
the neon sign, seen earlier, the camera pans down to
the door of the cafe. From inside we hear sounds of
music and laughter. The song is "It Had to Be You."*

Inside, Rick's is an expensive and chic nightclub which definitely possesses an air of sophistication and intrigue. The camera pans around the room soaking in the atmosphere. An orchestra is playing. The piano is a small, salmon-colored instrument on wheels. There is a Negro on the stool, playing and singing. About him there is a hum of voices, chatter and laughter. The occupants of the room are varied. There are Europeans in their dinner jackets, their women beautifully begowned and bejeweled. There are Moroccans in silk robes. Turks wearing fezzes. Levantines. Naval officers. Members of the Foreign Legion, distinguished by their kepis.

A customer in the cafe, seated at a table.

Man
Waiting, waiting, waiting. I'll never get out of here. I'll die in Casablanca.

A very well-dressed woman is talking to a Moor. She has a bracelet on her wrist, no other jewelry.

Woman
But can't you make it just a little more? Please.

Moor
I'm sorry, Madame, but diamonds are a drug on the market. Everybody sells diamonds. There are diamonds everywhere. Two thousand, four hundred.

Woman
distressed
All right.

Two conspirators are talking.

1st Man
The trucks are waiting, the men are waiting. Everything is . . .

He stops talking as two German officers walk by.

Two men are sitting at a table.

Man
It's the fishing smack Santiago. It leaves at one tomorrow
night, here from the end of La Medina. Third boat.

Refugee
Thank you, oh, thank you.

Man
And bring fifteen thousand francs in cash. Remember, in
cash.

*The camera dollies to the bar. As it passes the various
tables we hear a babel of foreign tongues. Here and there
we catch a scattered phrase or sentence in English. Now we
are at the bar. The Russian bartender is a friendly young
man. He hands a drink to a customer with the Russian
equivalent of "Bottoms Up." The customer answers with
"Cheerio."*

*Carl, the waiter, a fat, jovial German refugee with
spectacles is walking, tray in hand, to a private door, over
which a burly man stands guard.*

Carl
Open up, Abdul.

Abdul
respectfully, as he opens the door
Yes, Herr Professor.

*Carl goes into the gambling room. The camera takes in the
activity at the various tables. At one table two women are
glancing offscene at Rick's table. One of them calls to
Carl.*

Woman
Uh, waiter.

Carl
Yes, Madame?

Woman
Will you ask Rick if he'll have a drink with us?

41

Carl

Madame, he never drinks with customers. Never. I have
never seen him.

2nd Woman
disappointedly
What makes saloon-keepers so snobbish?

Man
to Carl
Perhaps if you told him I ran the second largest banking
house in Amsterdam.

Carl

The second largest? That wouldn't impress Rick. The leading banker in Amsterdam is now the pastry chef in our
kitchen.

Man
We have something to look forward to.

Carl
And his father is the bell boy.
laughs

*The overseer walks up to a table with a paper in his hand.
In the foreground at the table we see a drink and a man's
hand. The overseer places a check on the table. The man's
hand picks up the check and writes on it, in pencil: "Okay
—Rick." The overseer takes the check. The camera pulls
back to reveal Rick, sitting at a table alone playing
solitary chess. There is no expression on his face. Rick is
an American of indeterminate age. As people come into
the gambling room, he nods approval to Abdul. Several
people have just entered. The next man appears in the
doorway. Abdul looks to Rick who is glancing toward
the open door and indicating that the person seeking
admittance is not to be let in. Abdul starts to close the door
on the man.*

Abdul
I'm sorry sir, this is a private room.

German
Of all the nerve! Who do you think. . . ? I know there's gambling in there! There's no secret. You dare not keep me out of here!

The man tries to push his way through the door as Rick walks up.

Rick
coldly
Yes? What's the trouble?

Abdul
Er, this gentleman . . .

German
interrupting and waving his card
I've been in every gambling room between Honolulu and Berlin and if you think I'm going to be kept out of a saloon like this, you're very much mistaken.

At this moment, Ugarte tries to squeeze through the door-way blocked by the German. He gets through and passes Rick. He is a small, thin man with a nervous air. If he were an American, he would look like a tout.

Ugarte
Er, er, excuse me, please. Hello, Rick.

Rick just looks at the German calmly and takes the card out of the German's hand.

Rick
tearing up the card
Your cash is good at the bar.

German
What! Do you know who I am?

Rick
I do. You're lucky the bar's open to you.

German
This is outrageous. I shall report it to the Angriff!

The German storms off, tossing the pieces of his card into the air behind him. On his way back to his table, Rick meets Ugarte.

Ugarte
fawning
Huh. You know, Rick, watching you just now with the Deutsches Bank, one would think you'd been doing this all your life.

Rick
stiffening
Well, what makes you think I haven't?

Ugarte
vaguely
Oh, nothing. But when you first came to Casablanca, I thought . . .

Rick
coldly
You thought what?

Ugarte
fearing to offend Rick, laughs
What right do I have to think?
pulling out a chair at Rick's table
May I?
changing the subject
Too bad about those two German couriers, wasn't it?

Rick
indifferently
They got a lucky break. Yesterday they were just two German clerks; today they're the Honored Dead.

Ugarte
You are a very cynical person, Rick, if you'll forgive me for saying so.

44

Rick
shortly
I forgive you.

A waiter has just come up to the table with a tray of drinks.
He places one before Ugarte.

Ugarte
Er, thank you.
to Rick
Will you have a drink with me please?

Rick
No.

Ugarte
I forgot. You never drink with . . .
to waiter
I'll have another, please.
to Rick, sadly
You despise me, don't you?

Rick
indifferently
If I gave you any thought, I probably would.

Ugarte
But why? Oh, you object to the kind of business I do, huh?
But think of all those poor refugees who must rot in this
place if I didn't help them. That's not so bad. Through
ways of my own I provide them with exit visas.

Rick
For a price, Ugarte, for a price.

Ugarte
But think of all the poor devils who cannot meet Renault's
price. I get it for them for half. Is that so parasitic?

Rick
I don't mind a parasite. I object to a cut-rate one.

45

Ugarte

Well, Rick, after tonight I'll be through with the whole business, and I am leaving finally this Casablanca.

Rick

Who did you bribe for your visa? Renault or yourself?

Ugarte

ironically

Myself. I found myself much more reasonable.

he takes an envelope from his pocket and lays it on the table

Look, Rick, do you know what this is? Something that even you have never seen.

lowers his voice

Letters of transit signed by General deGaulle. [Marshal Weygand] Cannot be rescinded, not even questioned.

Rick looks at him, then holds out his hand for the envelope.

Ugarte

One moment. Tonight I'll be selling those for more money than even I have ever dreamed of, and then, addio Casablanca! You know, Rick, I have many friends in Casablanca, but somehow, just because you despise me you're the only one I trust. Will you keep these for me? Please.

Rick

For how long?

Ugarte

Perhaps an hour, perhaps a little longer.

Rick

taking them

I don't want them here overnight.

Ugarte

Don't be afraid of that. Please keep them for me. Thank you. I knew I could trust you.

46

Ugarte leaves the table just as the waiter comes up.

Ugarte
Oh, waiter. I'll be expecting some people. If anybody asks for me, I'll be right here.

Waiter
Yes, M'sieur.

The waiter leaves. Ugarte turns to Rick.

Ugarte
Rick, I hope you are more impressed with me now, huh? If you'll forgive me, I'll share my good luck with your roulette wheel.

He starts across the floor.

Rick
Just a moment.

Ugarte stops. Rick comes up to him.

Rick
Yeah, I heard a rumor that those German couriers were carrying letters of transit.

Ugarte doesn't reply for a moment.

Ugarte
Huh? I heard that rumor, too. Poor devils.

Rick looks at Ugarte steadily.

Rick
slowly
Yes, you're right, Ugarte. I am a little more impressed with you.

Rick starts for the door.

In the cafe, Sam is playing and singing the "Knock Wood" number, accompanied by the orchestra. The cafe is in

47

semi-darkness. The spotlight is on Sam, and every time the orchestra comes in on the "Knock Wood" business, the spotlight swings over to the orchestra. Rick makes his way from the gambling room to Sam on the floor. During one of the periods when the spotlight is on the orchestra, Rick slips the letters of transit into the piano.

Ferrari comes into the cafe, sits down and watches Sam in his number. He sees Rick. They smile at each other. At the end of the number, Ferrari goes to the bar to speak to Rick.

Ferrari
as he comes up to Rick
Hello, Rick.

Rick
Hello, Ferrari. How's business at the Blue Parrot?

Ferrari
Fine, but I would like to buy your cafe.

Rick
It's not for sale.

Ferrari
You haven't heard my offer.

Rick
It's not for sale at any price.

Ferrari
What do you want for Sam?

Rick
I don't buy or sell human beings.

Ferrari
That's too bad. That's Casablanca's leading commodity. In refugees alone we could make a fortune if you would work with me through the black market.

Rick
Suppose you run your business and let me run mine.
50

Ferrari

Suppose we ask Sam? Maybe he'd like to make a change.

Rick

Suppose we do.

Ferrari

My dear Rick, when will you realize that in this world today isolationism is no longer a practical policy?

Rick and Ferrari walk over to the piano.

Rick

Sam, Ferrari wants you to work for him at the Blue Parrot.

Sam

I like it fine here.

Rick

He'll double what I pay you.

Sam

Yeah, but I ain't got time to spend the money I make here.

Rick

Sorry, Ferrari.

At the long bar in the cafe proper, Yvonne is sitting on a stool drinking brandy. Sacha, who is looking at her with lovesick eyes, is filling her tumbler.

Sacha

The boss's private stock. Because, Yvonne, I loff you.

Yvonne
morosely
Oh, shut up.

Sacha
fondly
All right, all right. For you, Yvonne, I shot opp, because, Yvonne, I loff you. Uh oh.

Rick saunters into the scene, and leans against the bar next

*to Yvonne. He pays no attention to her. She looks at him
bitterly, without saying a word.*

Sacha
Oh, M'sieur Rick, M'sieur Rick. Some Germans, boom,
boom, boom, boom, gave this check. Is it all right?

*Rick looks the check over and tears it up. Yvonne, who
has never taken her eyes off Rick, finally blurts out:*

Yvonne
Where were you last night?

Rick
his back is to her
That's so long ago, I don't remember.

A pause

Yvonne
Will I see you tonight?

Rick
matter-of-factly
I never make plans that far ahead.

Yvonne turns, looks at Sacha, extends her glass to him.

Yvonne
Give me another.

Rick
Sacha, she's had enough.

Yvonne
Don't listen to him, Sacha. Fill it up.

Sacha
Yvonne, I loff you, but he pays me.

Yvonne wheels on Rick with drunken fury.

Yvonne
Rick, I'm sick and tired of having you . . .

Rick
Sacha, call a cab.

54

Sacha
Yes, boss.

Rick
taking Yvonne by the arm
Come on, we're going to get your coat.

Yvonne
Take your hands off me!

He pulls her along toward the hall door.

Rick
No. You're going home. You've had a little too much to drink.

On the street in front of Rick's Sacha stands at the curb signaling a cab. Finally one pulls up. Rick and Yvonne come out of the cafe. He is putting a coat over her shoulders. She is objecting violently.

Yvonne
Who do you think you are, pushing me around? What a fool I was to fall for a man like you.

Rick
to Sacha, as he and Yvonne approach the waiting cab
You'd better go with her, Sacha, to be sure she gets home.

Sacha
Yes, boss.

Rick
And come right back.

Sacha
his face falling
Yes, boss.

Rick is now standing outside the cafe, looking up at the revolving beacon light from the airport, which intermittently sheds its light on Rick's face. In the foreground, Renault is seated at a table on the cafe terrace.

Renault
Hello, Rick.

55

Rick
walking over to him
Hello, Louis.

Renault
How extravagant you are, throwing away women like that. Someday they may be scarce.

Rick sits down at the table.

Renault
his eyes are amused
You know, I think now I shall pay a call on Yvonne, maybe get her on the rebound, eh?

Rick
When it comes to women, you're a true democrat.

As they talk, Captain Tonelli and Lieutenant Casselle walk by to enter the cafe. Casselle is talking non-stop; Tonelli tries.

Renault
If he gets a word in it'll be a major Italian victory.

Rick laughs. There is the sound of an airplane on the adjacent airfield. Rick and Renault look in its direction. The plane takes off and flies directly over their heads.

Renault
The plane to Lisbon.
a pause
You would like to be on it?

Rick
curtly
Why? What's in Lisbon?

Renault
The clipper to America.

Rick doesn't answer. His look isn't a happy one.
58

Renault

I have often speculated on why you don't return to America. Did you abscond with the church funds? Did you run off with a senator's wife? I like to think you killed a man. It's the romantic in me.

Rick

still looking in the direction of the airport
It was a combination of all three.

Renault

And what in heaven's name brought you to Casablanca?

Rick

My health. I came to Casablanca for the waters.

Renault

Waters? What waters? We're in the desert.

Rick

I was misinformed.

Renault

Huh!

Emil, the croupier, comes out of the cafe and walks over to Rick.

Emil

Excuse me, M'sieur Rick, but a gentleman inside has won twenty thousand francs. The cashier would like some money.

Rick

not at all perturbed
Well, I'll get it from the safe.

Emil

I am so upset, M'sieur Rick. I do not understand how . . .

Rick

Forget it, Emil. Mistakes like that happen all the time.

The three men enter the cafe and walk through, passing Sam at the piano.

Renault
Rick, there's going to be some excitement here tonight. We are going to make an arrest in your cafe.

Rick
somewhat annoyed
What, again?

Renault
This is no ordinary arrest. A murderer, no less.

Rick's eyes react. Involuntarily, they glance toward the gambling room.

Renault
who has caught the look
If you are thinking of warning him, don't put yourself out. He cannot possibly escape.

Rick
I stick my neck out for nobody.

Renault
A wise foreign policy.

They start upstairs to Rick's office, passing Casselle who is still haranguing Tonelli.

Renault
You know, Rick, we could have made this arrest earlier in the evening at the Blue Parrot; but out of my high regard for you we are staging it here. It will amuse your customers.

Rick
Our entertainment is enough.

As Renault speaks, Rick is opening up the safe in a small dark room off the office. From the angle of the shot, only Rick's shadow can be seen, getting the money out.

60

Renault

Rick, we are to have an important guest tonight, Major Strasser of the Third Reich, no less. We want him to be here when we make the arrest. A little demonstration of the efficiency of my administration.

Rick

I see. And what's Strasser doing here? He certainly didn't come all the way to Casablanca to witness a demonstration of your efficiency.

Renault

Perhaps not.

Rick

giving the money to Emil
Here you are.

Emil

It shall not happen again, M'sieur.

Rick

That's all right.

Emil exits.

Rick

Louis, you've got something on your mind. Why don't you spill it?

Renault

admiringly
How observant you are. As a matter of fact, I wanted to give you a word of advice.

Rick

Yeah? Have a brandy?

Renault

Thank you. Rick, there are many exit visas sold in this cafe, but we know that you have never sold one. That is the reason we permit you to remain open.

Rick

amiably
I thought it was because we let you win at roulette.

Renault

Er, that is another reason. There is a man who's arrived in Casablanca on his way to America. He will offer a fortune to anyone who will furnish him with an exit visa.

Rick

Yeah? What's his name?

Renault

Victor Laszlo.

Rick

Victor Laszlo!

Renault

watching Rick's reaction

Rick, that is the first time I have ever seen you so impressed.

Rick

casual, again

Well, he's succeeded in impressing half the world.

Renault

It is my duty to see that he doesn't impress the other half.

now intensely serious

Rick, Laszlo must never reach America. He stays in Casablanca.

Rick

It'll be interesting to see how he manages.

Renault

Manages what?

Rick

His escape.

Renault

Oh, but I just told you . . .

Rick

Stop it. He escaped from a concentration camp and the

Nazis have been chasing him all over Europe.

Renault
This is the end of the chase.

Rick
Twenty thousand francs says it isn't.

They sit.

Renault
Is that a serious offer?

Rick
I just paid out twenty. I'd like to get it back.

Renault
Make it ten. I am only a poor corrupt official.

Rick
Okay.

Renault
Done. No matter how clever he is, he still needs an exit visa, or I should say, two.

Rick
Why two?

Renault
He is traveling with a lady.

Rick
He'll take one.

Renault
I think not. I have seen the lady. And if he did not leave her in Marseilles, or in Oran, he certainly won't leave her in Casablanca.

Rick
Maybe he's not quite as romantic as you are.

Renault

It doesn't matter. There is no exit visa for him.

Rick

Louis, whatever gave you the impression that I might be interested in helping Laszlo escape?

Renault

Because, my dear Ricky, I suspect that under that cynical shell you're at heart a sentimentalist.

Rick makes a face.

Renault

Oh, laugh if you will, but I happen to be familiar with your record. Let me point out just two items. In 1935 you ran guns to Ethiopia. In 1936, you fought in Spain on the Loyalists' side.

Rick

And got well paid for it on both occasions.

Renault

The winning side would have paid you much better.

Rick

Maybe.
changing the subject
Well, it seems you are determined to keep Laszlo here.

Renault

I have my orders.

Rick

Oh, I see. Gestapo spank.

Renault

My dear Ricky, you overestimate the influence of the Gestapo. I don't interfere with them and they don't interfere with me. In Casablanca I am master of my fate. I am captain of my . . .

He stops short as his aide enters and speaks.

64

Aide
Major Strasser is here, sir.

Rick
as Renault starts to leave
Yeah, you were saying . . . ?

Renault
hurriedly
Excuse me.

He hurries away. Rick smiles cynically.

Downstairs again, Renault walks up to Carl.

Renault
Carl, see that Major Strasser gets a good table, one close to the ladies.

Carl
I have already given him the best, knowing he is German and would take it anyway.

Renault walks over to one of his officers.

Renault
in a low voice
Take him quietly. Two guards at every door.

Officer
Yes, sir. Everything is ready, sir.

He salutes and goes off to speak to the guards. Rick has just come down the stairs. Renault walks over to Strasser's table.

Renault
Good evening, gentlemen.

Strasser
Good evening, Captain.

Heinze
Won't you join us?

Renault
sitting down

Thank you. It is a pleasure to have you here, Major.

Strasser
to the waiter
Er, champagne and a tin of caviar.

Renault
Er, may I recommend Veuve Cliquot '26, a good French wine.

Strasser
Thank you.

Waiter
Very well, sir.

Strasser
A very interesting club.

Renault
Especially so tonight, Major.
in a low voice
In a few minutes you will see the arrest of the man who murdered your couriers.

Strasser
I expected no less, Captain.

In the gambling room Ugarte is standing at the roulette table with his back to the camera. Two gendarmes approach him from behind.

Gendarme
Monsieur Ugarte?

Ugarte
looking around
Oh. Yes?

Gendarme
Will you please come with us.

Ugarte
Certainly. May I first please cash my chips?

The officer nods, the two follow Ugarte to the Cashier.

66

Ugarte
as he puts his chips through the window
Pretty lucky, huh? Two thousand, please.

At the door to the gambling room, two guards have just stationed themselves in case there is trouble.

Cashier
Two thousand.

Ugarte
Thank you.

Ugarte starts to walk out, followed by the gendarmes. At the doorway, he suddenly rushes through and slams the door behind him. By the time the gendarmes manage to get the door open again, Ugarte has pulled a gun. He fires at the doorway. The shots bring on pandemonium in the cafe. As Ugarte runs through the hallway he sees Rick, appearing from the opposite direction, and grabs him.

Ugarte
Rick! Rick, help me!

Rick
Don't be a fool. You can't get away.

Ugarte
Rick, hide me. Do something! You must help me, Rick. Do something!

Before he can finish, guards and gendarmes rush in and grab Ugarte. Rick stands impassive as they drag Ugarte off.

Ugarte
Rick! Rick!

Strasser
still seated at his table, to Renault
Excellent, Captain.

Rick is still standing where he was, as a customer walks by.

Man
half kiddingly, half earnest
When they come to get me, Rick, I hope you'll be more
of a help.

Rick
I stick my neck out for nobody.

*Rick comes out on the floor. An air of tense expectancy
pervades the room. A few customers are on the point of
leaving. Rick speaks in a very calm voice.*

Rick
I'm sorry there was a disturbance, folks, but it's all over
now. Everything's all right. Just sit down and have a good
time. Enjoy yourself.
glances toward Sam
All right, Sam.

Sam nods and begins to play.

*Renault, Strasser and Heinze are at their table. Rick walks
by.*

Renault
calling to Rick
Oh, Rick?

Rick stops and comes over to the table.

Renault
Rick, this is Major Heinrich Strasser of the Third Reich.

Strasser
How do you do, Mr. Rick?

Rick
Oh, how do you do?

Renault
And you already know Herr Heinze of the Third Reich.
68

Rick nods to Strasser and Heinze.

Strasser
Please join us, Mr. Rick.

Rick sits at the table.

Renault
We are very honored tonight, Rick. Major Strasser is one of the reasons the Third Reich enjoys the reputation it has today.

Strasser
smiling
You repeat "Third Reich" as though you expected there to be others.

Renault
Well, personally, Major, I will take what comes.

Strasser
to Rick
Do you mind if I ask you a few questions? Unofficially, of course.

Rick
Make it official, if you like.

Strasser
What is your nationality?

Rick
pokerface
I'm a drunkard.

Renault
That makes Rick a citizen of the world.

Rick
I was born in New York City if that'll help you any.

Strasser
amiably
I understand you came here from Paris at the time of the occupation.

Rick

There seems to be no secret about that.

Strasser

Are you one of those people who cannot *imagine* the Germans in their beloved Paris?

Rick

It's not particularly *my* beloved Paris.

Heinze

Can you imagine us in London?

Rick

When you get there, ask me.

Renault

Ho, diplomatist!

Strasser

How about New York?

Rick

Well, there are certain sections of New York, Major, that I wouldn't advise you to try to invade.

Strasser

Aha. Who do you think will win the war?

Rick

I haven't the slightest idea.

Renault

Rick is completely neutral about everything. And that takes in the field of women, too.

Strasser takes a little black book from his pocket and turns to a certain page.

Strasser

You weren't always so carefully neutral. We have a complete dossier on you.
reads
"Richard Blaine, American. Age, thirty-seven. Cannot return to his country."

74

looks up from the book
The reason is a little vague. We also know what you did in Paris, Mr. Blaine, and also we know why you left Paris.

Rick reaches over and takes the book from Strasser's hand.

Strasser
Don't worry. We are not going to broadcast it.

Rick
looking up from the book
Are my eyes really brown?

Strasser
You will forgive my curiosity, Mr. Blaine. The point is, an enemy of the Reich has come to Casablanca and we are checking up on anybody who can be of any help to us.

Rick
with a glance toward Renault
My interest in whether Victor Laszlo stays or goes is purely a sporting one.

Strasser
In this case, you have no sympathy for the fox?

Rick
Not particularly. I understand the point of view of the hound, too.

Strasser
Victor Laszlo published the foulest lies in the Prague newspapers until the very day we marched in, and even after that he continued to print scandal sheets in a cellar.

Renault
Of course, one must admit he has great courage.

Strasser
I admit he is very clever. Three times he slipped through our fingers. In Paris he continued his activities. We intend not to let it happen again.

Rick
rises with a slight smile

You'll excuse me, gentlemen. Your business is politics. Mine is running a saloon.

Strasser
Good evening, Mr. Blaine.

Rick walks away toward the gambling room.

Renault
You see, Major, you have nothing to worry about Rick.

Strasser
Perhaps.

At the entrance of the cafe, a couple is just coming in. They are Victor Laszlo and his companion, known as Miss Ilsa Lund. She wears a simple white gown. Her beauty is such that people turn to stare. The headwaiter comes up to them.

Headwaiter
Yes, M'sieur?

Laszlo
in quiet, even tones
I reserved a table. Victor Laszlo.

Headwaiter
Yes, M'sieur Laszlo. Right this way.

As the headwaiter takes them to a table, they pass by the piano, and the woman looks at Sam. The latter, with a conscious effort, keeps his eyes on the keyboard. The camera stops on Sam. After she has gone out of the scene, Sam steals a look in her direction. A man soon to be identified as Berger observes the couple. Strasser and Renault look up from their table. The headwaiter seats Ilsa. Laszlo takes the chair opposite. He surveys the room.

Laszlo
Two cointreaux, please.

Waiter
Yes, M'sieur.

Laszlo
to Ilsa
I saw no one of Ugarte's description.

Ilsa
Victor, I, I feel somehow we shouldn't stay here.

Laszlo
If we would walk out so soon, it would only call attention to us. Perhaps Ugarte's in some other part of the cafe.

A slight, middle-aged man, Berger, walks up to their table.

Berger
Excuse me, but you look like a couple who are on their way to America.

Laszlo
Well?

Berger takes a ring from his finger.

Berger
You will find a market there for this ring. I am forced to sell it at a great sacrifice.

Laszlo
Thank you, but I hardly think . . .

Berger
Then perhaps for the lady. The ring is quite unique.

He holds it down to their view. Carefully lifting up the stone, he reveals, on a gold plate in the setting underneath, an impression of the Lorraine Cross of General deGaulle.

Laszlo
Oh, yes, I'm *very* interested.

Berger
Good.

Laszlo
lower voice
What is your name?

Berger
Berger, Norwegian, and at your service, sir.

Laszlo
to Berger, in a low voice

I'll meet you in a few minutes at the bar.
in a louder voice, obviously for the benefit of someone offscene
I do not think we want to buy the ring. But thank you for showing it to us.

Berger takes the cue. He sighs and puts the ring away.

Berger
Such a bargain. But that is your decision?

Laszlo
I'm sorry. It is.

As Berger walks away, he brushes by Captain Renault who is approaching the table. He glances sharply at Berger as he passes. Then he beams toward the table.

Renault
Monsieur Laszlo, is it not?

Laszlo
Yes.

Renault
I am Captain Renault, Prefect of Police.

Laszlo
Yes. What is it you want?

Renault
amiably
Merely to welcome you to Casablanca and wish you a pleasant stay. It is not often we have so distinguished a visitor.

Laszlo
Thank you. You'll forgive me, Captain, but the present French administration has not always been so cordial. May I present Miss Ilsa Lund?

Renault
bows
I was informed you were the most beautiful woman ever to visit Casablanca. That was a gross understatement.

Ilsa's manner is friendly and reserved, her voice low and soft.

78

Ilsa
You are very kind.

Laszlo
Won't you join us?

Renault
If you will permit me.
calls to the waiter
Oh, Emil. Please, a bottle of your best champagne, and put it on my bill.

Emil
Very well, sir.

Laszlo
No, Captain, please.

Renault
No. Please, M'sieur, it is a little game we play. They put it on the bill, I tear the bill up. It is very convenient.

Ilsa laughs and glances off in Sam's direction.

Ilsa
Captain, the boy who is playing the piano, somewhere I have seen him.

Renault
Sam?

Ilsa
Yes.

Renault
He came from Paris with Rick.

Ilsa
Rick? Who's he?

Renault
smiling
Mademoiselle, you are in Rick's and Rick is, er . . .

Ilsa
Is what?

Renault
Well, Mademoiselle, he's the kind of a man that, well, if
I were a woman and *I* . . .
tapping his chest
. . . were not around, I should be in love with Rick. But
what a fool I am talking to a beautiful woman about
another man.

*Renault stops and looks off, then jumps to his feet as
Strasser enters.*

Renault
Er, excuse me. Ah, Major. Mademoiselle Lund, Monsieur
Laszlo, may I present Major Heinrich Strasser.

Strasser bows and smiles pleasantly.

Strasser
How do you do. This is a pleasure I have long looked
forward to.

*There is not the slightest recognition from either Ilsa or
Laszlo. Strasser waits to be asked to seat himself.*

Laszlo
I'm sure you'll excuse me if I am not gracious, but you
see, Major Strasser, I'm a Czechoslovakian.

Strasser
You were a Czechoslovakian. Now you are a subject of
the German Reich!

Laszlo
I've never accepted that privilege, and I'm now on French
soil.

Strasser
I should like to discuss some matters arising from your
presence on French soil.

Laszlo
This is hardly the time or the place.

Strasser
hardening
Then we shall state another time and another place. Tomorrow at ten in the Prefect's office, with Mademoiselle.
80

Laszlo

Captain Renault, I am under your authority. Is it your order that we come to your office?

Renault

amiably

Let us say that it is my request. That is a much more pleasant word.

Laszlo

Very well.

Renault and Strasser bow shortly.

Renault

Mademoiselle.

Strasser

Mademoiselle.

As they walk away.

Renault

to Strasser

A very clever tactical retreat, Major.

Strasser looks at Renault sharply, but sees only a non-committal smile on Renault's face.

At the table, Laszlo watches after Strasser and Renault.

Laszlo

This time they really mean to stop me.

Ilsa

Victor, I'm afraid for you.

Laszlo

We have been in difficult places before, haven't we?

Ilsa smiles back at him, but her eyes are still troubled.

On the floor, Corina strums a guitar and begins her number. Meanwhile, Laszlo looks about him with apparent casualness. He sees Strasser and Renault whispering together, then Berger.

Laszlo
I must find out what Berger knows.

Ilsa
Be careful.

Laszlo
I will, don't worry.

He rises and goes off. The camera closes in on Ilsa's troubled profile. While Corina is singing, Sam gives a worried glance in Ilsa's direction. Ilsa watches him.

At the bar, Berger is sipping a drink. Laszlo walks up, and casually takes a place at the bar next to Berger.

Laszlo
Mr. Berger, the ring, could I see it again?

Berger
Yes, M'sieur.

Laszlo
to Sacha
A champagne cocktail, please.

Laszlo takes the ring and looks at it.

Berger
in a low voice
I recognize you from the news photographs, M'sieur Laszlo.

Laszlo
In a concentration camp, one is apt to lose a little weight.

Berger
We read five times that you were killed in five different places.

Laszlo
smiles wryly
As you see, it was true every single time. Thank heaven I found you, Berger. I am looking for a man by the name of Ugarte. He is supposed to help me.

82

Berger
shakes his head silently
Ugarte cannot even help himself, M'sieur. He is under arrest for murder. He was arrested here tonight.

Laszlo
absorbs the shock quietly
I see.

Berger
with intense devotion
But we who are still free will do all we can. We are organized, M'sieur, underground like everywhere else. Tomorrow night there is a meeting at the Caverne du Roi. If you would come . . .

He stops as he sees Sacha bringing the drink to Laszlo.

Corina finishes her song.

At Laszlo's table, Ilsa sits alone.

Ilsa
to waiter
Will you ask the piano player to come over here, please?

Waiter
Very well, Mademoiselle.

Renault comes up to where Berger and Laszlo are sitting.

Renault
How's the jewelry business, Berger?

Berger
Er, not so good.
to Sacha
May I have my check, please?

Renault
Too bad you weren't here earlier, M'sieur Laszlo. We had quite a bit of excitement this evening, didn't we, Berger?

Berger
Er, yes. Excuse me, gentlemen.

Laszlo
My bill.

Renault
No. Two champagne cocktails, please.

Sacha
Yes, sir.

At Laszlo's table, Sam wheels in the piano. On his face is that funny fear. Ilsa herself is not as self-possessed as she tries to appear. There is something behind this, some mysterious, deep-flowing feeling.

Ilsa
Hello, Sam.

Sam
Hello, Miss Ilsa. I never expected to see you again.

He sits down and is ready to play.

Ilsa
It's been a long time.

Sam
Yes, ma'am. A lot of water under the bridge.

Ilsa
Some of the old songs, Sam.

Sam
Yes, ma'am.

Sam begins to play a number. He is nervous, waiting for anything.

Ilsa
Where is Rick?

Sam
evading
I don't know. I ain't seen him all night.

Sam looks very uncomfortable.

Ilsa
When will he be back?

86

Sam

Not tonight no more. He ain't coming. He went home.

Ilsa

Does he always leave so early?

Sam

Oh, he never . . . well . . .
desperately
he's got a girl up at the Blue Parrot. He goes up there all
the time.

Ilsa

You used to be a much better liar, Sam.

Sam

Leave him alone, Miss Ilsa. You're bad luck to him.

Ilsa
softly
Play it once, Sam, for old time's sake.

Sam

I don't know what you mean, Miss Ilsa.

Ilsa

Play it, Sam. Play "As Time Goes By."

Sam

I can't remember it, Miss Ilsa. I'm a little rusty on it.

*Of course he can. He doesn't want to play it. He seems
even more scared.*

Ilsa

I'll hum it for you.
starts to hum

He begins to play it very softly.

Ilsa

Sing it, Sam.

And Sam sings.

Sam

"You must remember this,
A kiss is just a kiss,

A sigh is just a sigh,
Etc."

The door to the gambling room opens. Rick comes swinging out. He has heard the music and he is livid. He walks briskly up to the piano.

Rick
Sam, I thought I told you never to play . . .

As he sees Ilsa, he stops abruptly, stops speaking, stops moving. Sam stops playing. Two close-ups reveal Ilsa and Rick seeing each other. Rick isn't breathing at all. It's a wallop, a shock. For a long moment he just looks at her and you can tell what he is thinking. Sam prepares to move the piano away.

Renault and Laszlo are approaching the table from the bar.

Renault
to Ilsa
Well, you were asking about Rick and here he is. Mademoiselle, may I present . . .

Rick
Hello, Ilsa.

Ilsa
Hello, Rick.

Renault
Oh, you've already met Rick, Mademoiselle?
no answer from either
Well then, perhaps you also . . .

Ilsa
This is Mr. Laszlo.

Laszlo
How do you do?

Rick
How do you do?

Laszlo
One hears a great deal about Rick in Casablanca.

Rick
looks back at him
And about Victor Laszlo everywhere.

Laszlo
Won't you join us for a drink?

Renault
laughing
Oh, no, Rick never . . .

Rick
Thanks. I will.

Renault
Well! A precedent is being broken. Er, Emil!

Laszlo
he is making conversation
This is a very interesting cafe. I congratulate you.

Rick
And I congratulate you.

Laszlo
What for?

Rick
Your work.

Laszlo
Thank you. I try.

Rick
We all try. You succeed.

Renault
I can't get over you two. She was asking about you earlier, Rick, in a way that made me extremely jealous.

Ilsa
to Rick
I wasn't sure you were the same. Let's see, the last time we met . . .

Rick
It was "La Belle Aurore."

Ilsa

How nice. You remembered. But of course, that was the day the Germans marched into Paris.

Rick

Not an easy day to forget.

Ilsa

No.

Rick

I remember every detail. The Germans wore gray, you wore blue.

Ilsa

Yes. I put that dress away. When the Germans march out, I'll wear it again.

Renault

Ricky, you're becoming quite human. I suppose we have to thank you for that, Mademoiselle.

Laszlo

Ilsa, I don't wish to be the one to say it, but it's late.

Renault

glancing at his wristwatch
So it is. And we have a curfew here in Casablanca. It would never do for the Chief of Police to be found drinking after hours and have to fine himself.

Rick and Ilsa look at each other.

Laszlo

signaling the waiter
I hope we didn't overstay our welcome.

Rick

Not at all.

Waiter

to Laszlo
Your check, sir.

Rick

takes check
Oh, it's my party.

90

Renault

Another precedent gone. This has been a very interesting evening. I'll call you a cab. Gasoline rationing, time of night.

Renault leaves.

Laszlo

We'll come again.

Rick

Anytime.

Ilsa

Say goodnight to Sam for me.

Rick

I will.

Ilsa

There's still nobody in the world who can play "As Time Goes By" like Sam.

Rick

He hasn't played it in a long time.

A pause. Ilsa smiles.

Ilsa

Goodnight.

Laszlo

Goodnight.

Rick

Goodnight.

Rick and Laszlo nod goodnight to each other. Laszlo and Ilsa start to the door, as Rick sits down again and stares off in their direction.

Ilsa and Laszlo are outside the cafe.

Laszlo

A very puzzling fellow, this Rick. What sort is he?

Ilsa doesn't look at him.

Ilsa
Oh, I really can't say, though I saw him quite often in Paris.

They join Renault at the curb.

Renault
Tomorrow at ten at the Prefect's office.

Laszlo
We'll be there.

Renault
Goodnight.

Ilsa
Goodnight.

Laszlo
Goodnight.

They get into the waiting cab, leaving Renault on the curb, smoking and looking bemused.

The cafe sign is just being turned off. The doorway is now illuminated only as the revolving beacon from the airport strikes it.

Inside the cafe, the customers have all gone. The house lights are out. Rick sits at a table. There is a glass of bourbon on the table directly in front of him, and another glass empty on the table before an empty chair. Near at hand is a bottle. Rick just sits. His face is entirely expressionless. The beacon light from the airport sweeps around the room creating a mood of unreality. Sam comes in. He stands hesitantly before Rick.

Sam
Boss.
no answer, as Rick drinks
Boss!

Rick
Yeah?

Sam
Boss, ain't you going to bed?

92

Rick
filling his glass
Not right now.

Sam realizes Rick is in a grim mood.

Sam
lightly, trying to kid Rick out of it
Ain't you planning on going to bed in the near future?

Rick
No.

Sam
You ever going to bed?

Rick
No.

Sam
still trying
Well, I ain't sleepy either.

Rick
Good. Then have a drink.

Sam
No. Not me, boss.

Rick
Then don't have a drink.

Sam
Boss, let's get out of here.

Rick
emphatically
No, sir. I'm waiting for a lady.

Sam
earnestly
Please, boss, let's go. Ain't nothing but trouble for you here.

Rick
She's coming back. I know she's coming back.

Sam

We'll take the car and drive all night. We'll get drunk. We'll go fishing and stay away until she's gone.

Rick

Shut up and go home, will you?

Sam

stubbornly

No, sir. I'm staying right here.

Sam sits down at the piano and starts to play softly.

Rick

really drunk now

They grab Ugarte and she walks in. Well, that's the way it goes. One in, one out.

pause as he thinks of something

Sam?

Sam

still playing

Yeah, boss?

Rick

Sam, if it's December 1941 in Casablanca, what time is it in New York?

Sam

Uh, my watch stopped.

Rick

drunken nostalgia

I bet they're asleep in New York. I'll bet they're asleep all over America.

pounds the table suddenly

Of all the gin joints in all the towns in all the world, she walks into mine!

irritably, to Sam

What's that you're playing?

Sam

who has been improvising

Just a little something of my own.

Rick

Well, stop it. You know what I want to hear.

94

Sam
No, I don't.
Rick
You played it for her and you can play it for me.
Sam
Well, I don't think I can remember it.
Rick
If she can stand it, I can. Play it!
Sam
Yes, boss.

Sam starts to play "As Time Goes By."
The camera closes in on Rick. From his expression we know that he is thinking of the past. Slowly the sounds of an orchestra join into Sam's playing as the scene dissolves.

It is Paris in spring. A shot of the Arc de Triomphe is followed by one of Rick driving a small, open car slowly along the boulevard. Close beside him, with her arm linked in his, sits Ilsa.

On an excursion boat on the Seine. At the rail of the boat stand Rick and Ilsa. They are transported by each other. Ilsa laughs.

Inside Rick's Paris apartment, Ilsa fixes flowers at the window. Rick opens champagne. Ilsa joins him.

Rick
Who are you really? And what were you before? What did you do and what did you think? Huh?
Ilsa
We said "no questions."
Rick
Here's looking at you, kid.

They drink.

Inside a swank Paris cafe, Rick and Ilsa dance.

Inside Ilsa's Paris apartment.
Ilsa
A franc for your thoughts.

Rick
In America they'd bring only a penny. I guess that's about all they're worth.
Ilsa
I'm willing to be overcharged. Tell me.

Rick
I was wondering.
Ilsa
Yes?

Rick
Why I'm so lucky. Why I should find you waiting for me to come along.

Ilsa
Why there is no other man in my life?
Rick
Uh huh.
Ilsa
That's easy. There was. He's dead.

Rick
Well, only one answer can take care of all our questions.

Ilsa
Well, only one question can take care of all our questions.
She kisses him.

Newsreel footage of the German occupation of France.

A man sells newspapers to people crowded around him. There is much excitement. Rick and Ilsa, sitting in a cafe, buy the newspaper and read it. Nearby, a group of frightened French people cluster around a loudspeaker wagon. A harsh voice is barking out the tragic news of the Nazi push toward Paris.
Rick
Nothing can stop them now. Wednesday, Thursday at the latest, they'll be in Paris.
Ilsa
frightened
Richard, they'll find out your record. It won't be safe for you here.

96

Rick

smiles

I'm on their blacklist already, their roll of honor.

A small cafe in the Montmartre. A shadow on the floor reflects the cafe sign "La Belle Aurore." Rick is at the bar getting glasses and a bottle of champagne. He walks over to Ilsa and Sam at the piano. Sam is playing "As Time Goes By." Ilsa's attitude, as she listens, is very distraught. There is evidently something on her mind, and it isn't all concerned with the war. Rick pours the champagne. His manner is wry, but not the bitter wryness we have seen in Casablanca.

Rick

Henri wants us to finish this bottle and then three more. He says he'll water his garden with champagne before he'll let the Germans drink any of it.

Sam

looking at his glass

This sort of takes the sting out of being occupied, doesn't it, Mr. Richard?

Rick

You said it!

to Ilsa

Here's looking at you, kid.

A loudspeaker is heard in the street. Rick and Ilsa look at each other, then hurry to the window. The loudspeaker is blaring in German.

Rick

My German's a little rusty.

Ilsa

sadly

It's the Gestapo. They say they expect to be in Paris tomorrow. They are telling us how to act when they come marching in.

smiling faintly

With the whole world crumbling, we pick this time to fall in love.

Rick

Yeah. It's pretty bad timing.

97

looks at her
Where were you, say, ten years ago?
Ilsa
trying to cheer up
Ten years ago? Let's see . . .
thinks
Yes. I was having a brace put on my teeth. Where were you?

Rick
Looking for a job.

Pause. Ilsa looks at him tenderly. Rick takes her in his arms, and kisses her hungrily. While they are locked in an embrace the dull boom of cannons is heard. Rick and Ilsa separate.

Ilsa
frightened, but trying not to show it
Was that cannon fire, or is it my heart pounding?
Rick
grimly
Ah, that's the new German 77. And judging by the sound, only about thirty-five miles away.
another booming is heard
And getting closer every minute. Here. Drink up. We'll never finish the other three.
Sam
The Germans'll be here pretty soon now, and they'll come looking for you. And don't forget there's a price on your head.
Ilsa reacts to this worriedly.
Rick
dryly
I left a note in my apartment. They'll know where to find me.

Ilsa looks at Rick.

Ilsa
Strange. I know so very little about you.

Rick
I know very little about you; just the fact that you had your teeth straightened.
98

Ilsa

But be serious, darling. You are in danger and you must leave Paris.

Rick

No, no, no, no. *We* must leave.

Ilsa

worried

Yes, of course, we.

Rick

The train for Marseilles leaves at five o'clock. I'll pick you up at your hotel at four-thirty.

Ilsa

quickly

No, no. Not at my hotel. I er, I have things to do in the city before I leave. I'll meet you at the station, huh?

Rick

All right. At a quarter to five.

a thought strikes him

Say, why don't we get married in Marseilles?

Ilsa

evasively

That's too far ahead to plan.

Rick

happy, excited at the thought of leaving with Ilsa

Yes, I guess it is a little too far ahead. Well, let's see. What about the engineer? Why can't he marry us on the train?

Ilsa

laughing nervously

Oh, darling!

Suddenly Ilsa starts to cry softly.

Rick

Well, why not? The captain on a ship can. It doesn't seem fair that . . . Hey, hey, what's wrong, kid?

Ilsa

controlling herself

I love you so much, and I hate this war so much.

stops, looks at Rick

Oh, it's a crazy world. Anything can happen. If you

99

shouldn't get away, I mean, if, if something should keep us apart, wherever they put you and wherever I'll be, I want you to know that I . . .

She can't go on. She lifts her face to his. He kisses her gently.

Ilsa

Kiss me. Kiss me as if it were the last time.

He looks into her eyes, then kisses her as though it were the last time. Her hand falls to the table, knocking over a glass. In the Gare de Lyon, there is a hectic, fevered excitement evident in the faces we pass. This is the last train from Paris! Rick appears in the crowd. He stops in front of the clock and puts his suitcase down. He glances at his watch. It is two minutes before train time. Rain is pouring over his head and shoulders, but he seems not to notice. He checks his watch again. Suddenly Sam appears.

Rick

Where is she? Have you seen her?

Sam

No, Mr. Richard. I can't find her. She checked out of the hotel. But this note came just after you left.

Sam pulls an envelope from his pocket. Rick grabs it, opens it, and stares down at the letter, which reads:

"Richard:

I cannot go with you or ever see you again. You must not ask why. Just believe that I love you. Go, my darling, and God bless you.

Ilsa"

The raindrops pour down the letter, smudging the writing. A whistle blows.

Sam

frantically

That's the last call, Mr. Richard, do you hear me? Come on, Mr. Richard. Let's get out of here. Come on, Mr. Richard, come on.

Sam pulls a stunned, reluctant Rick to the train. He looks back. The train starts to move just as he boards. From the steps, he looks off into the distance, then crumples the letter and tosses it away as the steam from the engine clouds over the scene.

When the haze clears, there is a close-up of a glass on the

100

table in the cafe. Rick's hand reaches for it and knocks it over. The camera pans to Rick's face. He is drunk. Sam walks over to the table to pick up the glass and a fallen chair. Just then the door opens and Ilsa is there. Rick is staring at the doorway. Ilsa lingers a moment, then moves over to the table.

Ilsa

Rick, I have to talk to you.

Her manner is a little uncertain, a little tentative, but with a quiet determination beneath it.

Rick

Oh. I saved my first drink to have with you. Here.

Ilsa

No. No, Rick. Not tonight.

Rick

Especially tonight.

She sits down in the chair before the empty glass. Her eyes are searching his face, but there is no expression on it except a cold and impassive one. Reaching for the bottle, he pours himself another drink.

Ilsa

Please.

Rick

Why did you have to come to Casablanca? There are other places.

Ilsa

I wouldn't have come if I had known that you were here. Believe me, Rick, it's true. I didn't know.

Rick

It's funny about your voice, how it hasn't changed. I can still hear it. "Richard dear, I'll go with you anyplace. We'll get on a train together and never stop."

Ilsa

Please don't. Don't, Rick! I can understand how you feel.

Rick

Huh! You understand how I feel. How long was it we had, honey?

Ilsa

I didn't count the days.

Rick

Well, I did. Every one of them. Mostly I remember the

101

last one. A wow finish. A guy standing on a station plat-
form in the rain with a comical look on his face, because
his insides had been kicked out.

He takes a drink.

Ilsa

after a pause

Can I tell you a story, Rick?

Rick

Has it got a wow finish?

Ilsa

I don't know the finish yet.

Rick

Well, go on, tell it. Maybe one will come to you as you
go along.

Ilsa

It's about a girl who had just come to Paris from her home
in Oslo. At the house of some friends she met a man
about whom she'd heard her whole life, a very great and
courageous man. He opened up for her a whole beautiful
world full of knowledge and thoughts and ideals. Everything she knew or ever became was because of him. And
she looked up to him and worshipped him with a feeling
she supposed was love.

Rick

Yes, that's very pretty. I heard a story once. As a matter of
fact, I've heard a lot of stories in my time. They went
along with the sound of a tinny piano playing in the parlor
downstairs. "Mister, I met a man once when I was a kid,"
it'd always begin.

pause

Huh. I guess neither one of our stories was very funny.
Tell me, who was it you left me for? Was it Laszlo, or were
there others in between? Or aren't you the kind that tells?

*Ilsa, shuddering, gets up and leaves. Rick's head slumps
over the table.*

*The next morning in Renault's office, Strasser is with
Renault.*

Strasser

I strongly suspect that Ugarte left the letters of transit
with Mr. Blaine. I would suggest you search the cafe immediately and thoroughly.

103

Renault

If Rick has the letters, he's much too smart to let you find them there.

Strasser

You give him credit for too much cleverness. My impression was that he's just another blundering American.

Renault

But we mustn't underestimate American blundering.

innocently

I was with them when they "blundered" into Berlin in 1918.

Strasser looks at him.

Strasser

As to Laszlo, we want him watched twenty-four hours a day.

Renault

reassuringly

It may interest you to know that at this very moment he is on his way here.

Laszlo and Ilsa make their way through the jam in the lobby of the Prefecture. Jan and Annina are there, talking to an officer.

Officer

to Jan and Annina

There's nothing we can do.

Laszlo and Ilsa enter Renault's office. He bows to them both.

Renault

I am delighted to see you both. Did you have a good night's rest?

Laszlo

I slept very well.

Renault

That's strange. Nobody is supposed to sleep well in Casablanca.

Laszlo

briefly

May we proceed with the business?

104

Renault
With pleasure. Won't you sit down?

Laszlo
Thank you.

Strasser
now as cold as Laszlo
Very well, Herr Laszlo, we will not mince words. You
are an escaped prisoner of the Reich. So far you have
been fortunate enough in eluding us. You have reached
Casablanca. It is my duty to see that you stay in Casablanca.

Laszlo
Whether or not you succeed is, of course, problematical.

Strasser
Not at all. Captain Renault's signature is necessary on every
exit visa.
turns to Renault
Captain, would you think it is possible that Herr Laszlo
will receive a visa?

Renault
I am afraid not. My regrets, M'sieur.

Laszlo
Well, perhaps I shall like it in Casablanca.

Strasser
And Mademoiselle?

Ilsa
You needn't be concerned about me.

Laszlo
prepares to rise
Is that all you wish to tell us?

Strasser
Don't be in such a hurry. You have all the time in the
world. You may be in Casablanca indefinitely . . .
suddenly leans forward, speaks intently
. . . or you may leave for Lisbon tomorrow, on one condition.

105

Laszlo
And that is?

Strasser
You know the leaders of the underground movement in
Paris, in Prague, in Brussels, in Amsterdam, in Oslo, in
Belgrade, in Athens.

Laszlo
Even in Berlin.

Strasser
Yes, even in Berlin. If you will furnish me with their
names and their exact whereabouts, you will have your
visa in the morning.

Renault
tongue in cheek again
And the honor of having served the Third Reich!

Laszlo
I was in a German concentration camp for a year. That's
honor enough for a lifetime.

Strasser
You will give us the names?

Laszlo
If I didn't give them to you in a concentration camp where
you had more "persuasive methods" at your disposal, I
certainly won't give them to you now.
*the passionate conviction in his voice now revealing the
crusader*
And what if you track down these men and kill them?
What if you murdered all of us? From every corner of
Europe, hundreds, thousands, would rise to take our places.
Even Nazis can't kill that fast.

Strasser
Herr Laszlo, you have a reputation for eloquence which I
can now understand. But in one respect you are mistaken.
You said the enemies of the Reich could all be replaced,
but there is one exception. No one could take your place
in the event anything unfortunate should occur to you
while you were trying to escape.

108

Laszlo

You won't dare to interfere with me here. This is still unoccupied France. Any violation of neutrality would reflect on Captain Renault.

Renault

M'sieur, insofar as it is in my power . . .

Laszlo

Thank you.

Renault

By the way, M'sieur, last night you evinced an interest in Signor Ugarte.

Laszlo

Yes.

Renault

I believe you have a message for him?

Laszlo

Nothing important, but may I speak to him now?

Strasser

wryly

You would find the conversation a trifle one-sided. Signor Ugarte is dead.

Close-ups of Ilsa, then Laszlo, reveal their disappointment. Strasser observes.

Ilsa

Oh.

Renault

holding the report

I am making out the report now. We haven't quite decided whether he committed suicide or died trying to escape.

Laszlo

Are you quite finished with us?

Strasser

For the time being.

Laszlo
Good day.

As Ilsa and Laszlo leave, an officer comes in. When the door has closed on Ilsa and Laszlo, Renault speaks to Strasser.

Renault
Undoubtedly their next step will be to the black market.

Officer
Excuse me, Captain. Another visa problem has come up.

Renault
happily, as he looks at himself in the mirror
Show her in.

Officer
Yes, sir.

The black market is a cluttered Arab street of bazaars, shops and stalls. All kinds and races of people are milling about the merchandise which native dealers have on outdoor display. Both men and women are dressed in tropical clothes. The canopies over the stalls give them some protection from the scorching sun. On the surface, the atmosphere is merely languid, but there is the sinister undercurrent of illicit trade.

A Frenchman and a native are talking together in low tones.

Native
I'm sorry, M'sieur, we would have to handle the police. This is a job for Signor Ferrari.

Man
Ferrari?

Native
It can be most helpful to know Signor Ferrari. He's pretty near got a monopoly on the black market here. You will find him over there at the Blue Parrot.

Man
Thanks.

Outside the cafe, a blue parrot sits on a perch. Inside, the cafe is much less pretentious than Rick's, but well populated. Rick enters and walks through the cafe toward Ferrari's office just as Ferrari is emerging with Jan and Annina, who look very downhearted.

Ferrari
There, don't be too downhearted. Perhaps you can come to terms with Captain Renault.

Jan
Thank you very much, Signor.

He leads Annina away. Rick is behind Ferrari and calls out to him.

Rick
Hello, Ferrari.

Signor Ferrari turns around, pleased to see Rick.

Ferrari
Ah, good morning, Rick.

Rick
I see the bus is in. I'll take my shipment with me.

Ferrari
No hurry. I'll have it sent over. Have a drink with me.

Rick
I never drink in the morning. And every time you send my shipment over, it's always just a little bit short.

Ferrari
chuckling
Carrying charges, my boy, carrying charges. Here, sit down. There's something I want to talk over with you, anyhow.
hailing a waiter
The bourbon.
to Rick, sighing deeply
The news about Ugarte upset me very much.

111

Rick

You're a fat hypocrite. You don't feel any sorrier for Ugarte than I do.

Ferrari
eyes Rick closely
Of course not. What upsets me is the fact that Ugarte is dead and no one knows where those letters of transit are.

Rick
dead-pan
Practically no one.

Ferrari

If I could lay my hands on those letters, I could make a fortune.

Rick

So could I. And I'm a poor businessman.

Ferrari

I have a proposition for whoever has those letters. I will handle the entire transaction, get rid of the letters, take all the risk, for a small percentage.

Rick

And the carrying charges?

Ferrari
smiling
Naturally there will be a few incidental expenses.
looking at Rick squarely
That is the proposition I have for whoever has those letters.

Rick
dryly
I'll tell him when he comes in.

Ferrari

Rick, I'll put my cards on the table. I think you know where those letters are.

114

Rick

Well, you're in good company. Renault and Strasser probably think so, too.

looks out of the window to see Laszlo walking toward the cafe leaving Ilsa at the linen bazaar

That's why I came over here to give them a chance to ransack my place.

Ferrari

Rick, don't be a fool. Take me into your confidence. You need a partner.

Rick isn't listening to him. He is looking through the open window in the direction of the linen bazaar.

Rick

getting up

Excuse me, I'll be getting back.

Laszlo reaches the entrance to the cafe as Rick is coming out. He stops and addresses Rick politely.

Laszlo

Good morning.

Rick

Signor Ferrari is the fat gent at the table.

As he exits, Laszlo looks after him with a puzzled expression.

At the linen stall, Ilsa is examining a tablecloth which an Arab vendor is endeavoring to sell. He is holding a sign which reads "700 francs."

Arab

You will not find a treasure like this in all Morocco, Mademoiselle. Only seven hundred francs.

Rick walks up behind Ilsa.

Rick

You're being cheated.

She looks briefly at Rick, then turns away. Her manner is politely formal.

Ilsa

It doesn't matter, thank you.

Arab

Ah, the lady is a friend of Rick's? For friends of Rick we have a small discount. Did I say seven hundred francs? You can have it for two hundred.

Reaching under the counter, he takes out a sign reading, "200 francs" and replaces the other sign with it.

Rick

I'm sorry I was in no condition to receive you when you called on me last night.

Ilsa

It doesn't matter.

Arab

Ah, for *special* friends of Rick's we have a *special* discount. One hundred francs.

He replaces the second sign with a third which reads, "100 francs."

Rick

Your story had me a little confused. Or maybe it was the bourbon.

Arab

I have some tablecloths, some napkins . . .

Ilsa

Thank you. I'm really not interested.

118

Arab
Please, one minute. Wait!
hurriedly exits

Ilsa pretends to examine the goods on the counter.

Rick
Why did you come back? To tell me why you ran out on me at the railway station?

Ilsa
quietly
Yes.

Rick
Well, you can tell me now. I'm reasonably sober.

Ilsa
I don't think I will, Rick.

Rick
Why not? After all, I got stuck with a railway ticket. I think I'm entitled to know.

Ilsa
slowly
Last night I saw what has happened to you. The Rick I knew in Paris, I could tell him. He'd understand. But the one who looked at me with such hatred . . . well, I'll be leaving Casablanca soon and we'll never see each other again.
now looking at him
We knew very little about each other when we were in love in Paris. If we leave it that way, maybe we'll remember those days and not Casablanca, not last night.

Rick
his voice low but intense
Did you run out on me because you couldn't take it? Because you knew what it would be like, hiding from the police, running away all the time?

Ilsa
You can believe that if you want to.

Rick
Well, I'm not running away any more. I'm settled now, above a saloon, it's true, but . . .
ironically
Walk up a flight. I'll be expecting you.

Ilsa turns her head away.

Rick
All the same, someday you'll lie to Laszlo. You'll be there!

Ilsa
No, Rick, no. You see, Victor Laszlo is my husband.

Rick stares at her.

Ilsa
And was, even when I knew you in Paris.

She walks away into the cafe as Rick stares after her.

Inside, Ilsa sits with Laszlo and Ferrari.

Ferrari
I was just telling M'sieur Laszlo that, unfortunately, I am not able to help him.

Ilsa
troubled
Oh.

Laszlo
You see, my dear, the word has gone around.

Ferrari
to Ilsa
As leader of all illegal activities in Casablanca, I am an influential and respected man. It would not be worth my

120

life to do anything for M'sieur Laszlo. You, however, are a different matter.

Laszlo
Signor Ferrari thinks it might just be possible to get an exit visa for you.

Ilsa
You mean for me to go on alone?

Ferrari
And *only* alone.

Laszlo
I will stay here and keep on trying. I'm sure in a little while . . .

Ferrari
We might as well be frank, M'sieur. It will take a miracle to get you out of Casablanca. And the Germans have outlawed miracles.

Ilsa
to Ferrari
We are only interested in two visas, Signor.

Laszlo
Please, Ilsa, don't be hasty.

Ilsa
firmly
No, Victor, no.

Ferrari
You two will want to discuss this. Excuse me. I'll be at the bar.

Ferrari gets to his feet and walks away.

Laszlo
No, Ilsa, I won't let you stay here. You must get to

121

America. And believe me, somehow I will get out and join you.

Ilsa
But, Victor, if the situation were different, if I had to stay and there were only a visa for one, would you take it?

Laszlo hesitates.

Laszlo
not very convincingly
Yes, I would.

Ilsa smiles faintly.

Ilsa
Yes, I see. When I had trouble getting out of Lille, why didn't you leave me there? And when I was sick in Marseilles and held you up for two weeks and you were in danger every minute of the time, why didn't you leave me then?

Laszlo
with a wry smile
I meant to, but something always held me up.
reaches over, puts his hand over hers
I love you very much, Ilsa.

Ilsa
smiling
Your secret will be safe with me. Ferrari is waiting for our answer.

At the bar Ferrari is talking to a waiter.

Ferrari
Not more than fifty francs though.

Ilsa and Laszlo walk up to him.
122

Laszlo

We've decided, Signor Ferrari. For the present we'll go on looking for two exit visas. Thank you very much.

Ferrari

Well, good luck. But be careful.
a flick of his eyes in the direction of the bazaar
You know you're being shadowed?

Laszlo

glancing in the direction of the bazaar
Of course. It becomes an instinct.

Ferrari

shrewdly looking at Ilsa
I observe that you in one respect are a very fortunate man, M'sieur. I am moved to make one more suggestion, why, I do not know, because it cannot possibly profit me, but, have you heard about Signor Ugarte and the letters of transit?

Laszlo

Yes, something.

Ferrari

Those letters were not found on Ugarte when they arrested him.

Laszlo

after a moment's pause
Do you know where they are?

Ferrari

Not for sure, M'sieur, but I will venture to guess that Ugarte left those letters with M'sieur Rick.

Ilsa's face darkens. Laszlo quietly observes.

Laszlo
Rick?

Ferrari

He is a difficult customer, that Rick. One never knows what he'll do or why. But it is worth a chance.

Laszlo

Thank you very much. Good day.

Ilsa

Goodbye, thank you for your coffee, Signor. I shall miss that when we leave Casablanca.

Ferrari

bows

It was gracious of you to share it with me. Good day, Mademoiselle, M'sieur.

Laszlo

Good day.

As Ilsa and Laszlo leave the cafe, Ferrari nonchalantly swats a fly on a table.

Outside Rick's cafe, the sign is lit up and the sounds of music filter out into the air. Inside at the bar, the dark European has found another tourist.

Dark European

Here's to you, sir.

Tourist

Er, good luck, yes.

Dark European

I'd better be going.

Tourist

Er, my check, please.

Dark European

I have to warn you, sir. I beseech you . . .

The tourist laughs nervously. The dark European picks his pocket.

124

Dark European
This is a dangerous place, full of vultures. Vultures everywhere! Thanks for everything.

Tourist
laughing
Er, goodbye, sir.

Dark European
It has been a pleasure to meet you.
dashing off and colliding with Carl
Oh, I'm sorry.

As the dark European hurries away, Carl checks all his pockets to make sure nothing is missing.

Sam and Corina finish their number. Strasser and his crowd enter the cafe and pass Rick's table. Carl brings Rick a bottle and glass.

Carl
M'sieur Rick, you are getting to be your best customer.

Carl exits; Renault comes up to Rick.

Renault
Well, Ricky. I'm very pleased with you. Now you're beginning to live like a Frenchman.

Rick
That was some going-over your men gave my place this afternoon. We just barely got cleaned up in time to open.

Renault
Well, I told Strasser he wouldn't find the letters here. But I told my men to be especially destructive. You know how that impresses Germans? Rick, have you got these letters of transit?

Rick
steadily
Louis, are you pro-Vichy or Free French?

125

Renault
promptly
Serves me right for asking a direct question. The subject is closed.

Rick
Well, it looks like you're a little late.

Renault
Huh?

Rick is gazing at Yvonne and a German officer approaching the bar.

Rick
So Yvonne's gone over to the enemy.

Renault
Who knows? In her own way she may constitute an entire second front.
gets up
I think it's time for me to flatter Major Strasser a little. I'll see you later, Rick.
he strolls away.

At the bar, Yvonne and the German officer place their order.

Yvonne
Sacha!

German Officer
French seventy-fives.

Yvonne
somewhat tight already
Put up a whole row of them, Sacha . . .
indicating on the bar with her hand
. . . starting here and ending here.

German Officer
cutting in
We will begin with two.

A French officer at the bar makes a remark to Yvonne.
126

French Officer
in French
Say, you, you are not French to go with a German like this!

Yvonne
in French
What are you butting in for?

French Officer
in French
I am butting in . . .

Yvonne
breaking in, in French
It's none of your business!

German Officer
in French
No, no, no, no! One minute!
in English
What did you say? Would you kindly repeat it?

French Officer
What I said is none of your business!

German Officer
I will make it my business!

They begin to fight.

Yvonne
in French
Stop! I beg of you! I beg of you, stop!

There are exclamations from people nearby. German of-ficers at a table rise, ready to join in. Rick walks up and separates the two men.

Rick
to the German
I don't like disturbances in my place. Either lay off politics or get out.

127

French Officer
in French
Dirty Boche. Someday we'll have our revenge!

At Strasser's table, Renault, Strasser and the others sit down again.

Strasser
You see, Captain, the situation is not as much under control as you believe.

Renault
My dear Major, we are trying to cooperate with your government, but we cannot regulate the feelings of our people.

Strasser
eyes him closely
Captain Renault, are you entirely certain which side you're on?

Renault
I have no conviction, if that's what you mean. I blow with the wind, and the prevailing wind happens to be from Vichy.

Strasser
And if it should change?

Renault
smiles
Surely the Reich doesn't admit that possibility?

Strasser
We are concerned about more than Casablanca. We know that every French province in Africa is honeycombed with traitors waiting for their chance, waiting, perhaps, for a leader.

Renault
casually
A leader, like Laszlo?

128

Strasser
Uh huh. I have been thinking. It is too dangerous if we let him go. It may be too dangerous if we let him stay.

Renault
thoughtfully
I see what you mean.

Carl approaches the Leuchtags' table with a bottle. They are a middle-aged couple.

Carl
in German
I brought you the finest brandy. Only the employees drink it here.

Mr. Leuchtag
Thank you, Carl.

Carl
as he pours
For Mrs. Leuchtag.

Mrs. Leuchtag
Thank you, Carl.

Carl
For Mr. Leuchtag.

Mr. Leuchtag
Carl, sit down. Have a brandy with us.

Mrs. Leuchtag
beaming with happiness
To celebrate our leaving for America tomorrow.

Carl
sitting
Thank you very much. I thought you would ask me, so I brought the good brandy and a third glass.

129

Mrs. Leuchtag
At last the day has came.

Mr. Leuchtag
Frau Leuchtag and I are speaking nothing but English now.

Mrs. Leuchtag
So we should feel at home ven ve get to America.

Carl
A very nice idea.

Mr. Leuchtag
raising his glass
To America.

Mrs. Leuchtag and Carl repeat "To America." *They clink glasses and drink.*

Mr. Leuchtag
Liebchen, uh, sweetness heart, what watch?

Mrs. Leuchtag
glancing at her wristwatch
Ten watch.

Mr. Leuchtag
surprised
Such much?

Carl
Er, you will get along beautifully in America, huh.

Coming from the gambling room, Annina meets Renault in the hallway.

Renault
How's lady luck treating you? Aw, too bad. You'll find him over there.

Annina sees Rick and goes to his table.

132

Annina
M'sieur Rick?

Rick
Yes?

Annina
Could I speak to you for just a moment, please?

Rick looks at her.

Rick
How did you get in here? You're under age.

Annina
I came with Captain Renault.

Rick
cynically
I should have known.

Annina
My husband is with me, too.

Rick
He is? Well, Captain Renault's getting broadminded. Sit down. Will you have a drink?

Annina shakes her head.

Rick
No, of course not. Do you mind if I do?

Annina
No.
nervously, as Rick pours himself a drink
M'sieur Rick, what kind of man is Captain Renault?

Rick
Oh, he's just like any other man, only more so.

Annina

No, I mean, is he trustworthy? Is his word . . .

Rick

Now, just a minute. Who told you to ask me that?

Annina

He did. Captain Renault did.

Rick

I thought so. Where's your husband?

Annina

At the roulette table, trying to win enough for our exit visa. Of course, he's losing.

Rick looks at her closely.

Rick

How long have you been married?

Annina

simply

Eight weeks. We come from Bulgaria. Oh, things are very bad there, M'sieur. A devil has the people by the throat. So Jan and I, we, we do not want our children to grow up in such a country.

Rick

wearily

So you decided to go to America.

Annina

Yes, but we have not much money, and travelling is so expensive and difficult. It was much more than we thought to get here. And then Captain Renault sees us and he is so kind. He wants to help us.

Rick

Yes, I'll bet.

134

Annina

He tells me he can give us an exit visa, but we have no money.

Rick

Does he know that?

Annina

Oh, yes.

Rick

And he is still willing to give you a visa?

Annina

Yes, M'sieur.

Rick

And you want to know . . .

Annina

Will he keep his word?

Rick

looking at his drink
He always has.

There is a silence. Annina is very disturbed.

Annina

Oh, M'sieur, you are a man. If someone loved you very much, so that your happiness was the only thing that she wanted in the whole world, but she did a bad thing to make certain of it, could you forgive her?

Rick

staring off into space
Nobody ever loved me that much.

Annina

And he never knew, and the girl kept this bad thing locked in her heart? That would be all right, wouldn't it?

135

Rick
harshly
You want my advice?

Annina
Oh, yes, please.

Rick
Go back to Bulgaria.

Annina
Oh, but if you knew what it means to us to leave Europe, to get to America! Oh, but if Jan should find out! He is such a boy. In many ways I am so much older than he is.

Rick
Yes, well, everybody in Casablanca has problems. Yours may work out. You'll excuse me.

Rick gets up and leaves Annina at the table.

Annina
tonelessly
Thank you, M'sieur.

She remains seated.

Rick is checking the reservation list at the desk when he sees Ilsa and Laszlo enter the cafe. He comes up to them.

Rick
Good evening.

Laszlo
Good evening. You see, here we are again.

Rick
I take that as a great compliment to Sam.
to Ilsa
I suppose he means to you Paris of, well, happier days.
136

Ilsa
quietly
He does. Could we have a table close to him?

Laszlo
who has been looking around
And as far from Major Strasser as possible.

Rick
Well, the geography might be a little difficult to arrange.
snaps his fingers for the headwaiter
Paul! Table thirty!

Headwaiter
to Ilsa and Laszlo
Yes, sir. Right this way, if you please.

Rick
to Ilsa
I'll have Sam play "As Time Goes By." I believe that's your favorite tune.

Ilsa
smiling
Thank you.

Rick walks over to Sam and whispers something to him. Sam stops what he is playing and begins "As Time Goes By," shaking his head. Laszlo orders.

Laszlo
Two cognacs, please.

Rick goes to the gambling room. Inside, at the roulette table, Jan's eyes are tragic. He has only three chips left. He seems bewildered. As Rick comes up, the croupier is speaking to Jan:

Croupier
Do you wish to place another bet, sir?

Jan
No, no, I guess not.

Rick stands behind Jan.

Rick
to Jan, dead-pan
Have you tried twenty-two tonight? I said, twenty-two.

*Jan looks at Rick, then at the chips in his hand. A pause.
He puts the chips on twenty-two.*

*Rick and the croupier exchange looks. The croupier un-
derstands what Rick wants him to do. He spins the wheel.
In the background, Carl is looking at the wheel, fascinated.
The wheel stops spinning.*

Croupier
calling out in French
Twenty-two, black, twenty-two.

*The croupier pushes a pile of chips onto the number. Jan
reaches for it. Renault, at a nearby table, takes notice of
what is happening.*

Rick
not even looking at Jan
Leave it there.

*Jan hesitates, then withdraws his hands. In the background,
Carl draws a little closer. The wheel spins. Nobody speaks
while it spins. It stops.*

Croupier
Twenty-two, black.

*In the background, Carl gasps. The croupier shoves a pile
of chips toward Jan. Renault looks miffed.*

Rick
to Jan
Cash it in and don't come back.
138

A customer complains to Carl.

Customer
Say, you sure this place is honest?

Carl
fervently
Honest! As honest as the day is long!

While Jan and Annina cash their chips, Rick speaks to the croupier.

Rick
How we doing tonight?

Croupier
dryly
Well, a couple of thousand less than I thought there would be.

Rick smiles slightly and exits toward the bar. Annina runs up to him and hugs him.

Annina
M'sieur Rick, I . . .

Rick
He's just a lucky guy.

Carl
solicitously
M'sieur Rick, may I get you a cup of coffee?

Rick
No thanks, Carl.

Carl
M'sieur Rick!

Renault seeing that Jan has won, gets up from his table to follow Rick. Jan and Annina stop him on the way.

139

Jan

Captain Renault, may I . . . ?

Renault

Oh, not here, please. Come to my office in the morning.
We'll do everything business-like.

Jan

We'll be there at six.

Renault

I'll be there at ten.
smiling insincerely
I am very happy for both of you. Still, it's strange that you
won.
he looks off and sees Rick
Well, maybe not so strange. I'll see you in the morning.

Annina

Thank you so much, Captain Renault.

*At the bar, Carl whispers in Sacha's ear. Sacha says "No!"
He runs to Rick.*

Sacha

Boss, you've done a beautiful thing.

He kisses Rick on both cheeks.

Rick

Go away, you crazy Russian!

*Carl pours a brandy for Rick. Pretending not to do so,
Rick is glancing in Ilsa's direction. Renault comes up to
him.*

Renault

As I suspected, you're a rank sentimentalist.

Rick

Yeah? Why?
140

Renault
chidingly
Why do you interfere with my little romances?

Rick
Put it down as a gesture to love.

Renault
good-naturedly
Well, I forgive you this time. But I'll be in tomorrow night with a breathtaking blonde, and it will make me very happy if she loses. Uh huh!

He smiles and walks off toward the gambling room. Laszlo comes up to Rick.

Laszlo
M'sieur Blaine, I wonder if I could talk to you?

Rick
Go ahead.

Laszlo
Well, isn't there some other place? It's rather confidential, what I have to say.

Rick
My office.

Laszlo
Right.

In the office.

Laszlo
You must know it's very important I get out of Casablanca.
simply
It's my privilege to be one of the leaders of a great movement. You know what I have been doing. You know what it means to the work, to the lives of thousands and thou-

141

sands of people that I be free to reach America and continue my work.

Rick

I'm not interested in politics. The problems of the world are not in my department. I'm a saloon keeper.

Laszlo

My friends in the underground tell me that you have quite a record. You ran guns to Ethiopia. You fought against the fascists in Spain.

Rick

What of it?

Laszlo

Isn't it strange that you always happened to be fighting on the side of the underdog?

Rick

Yes. I found that a very expensive hobby, too. But then I never was much of a businessman.

Laszlo

Are you enough of a businessman to appreciate an offer of a hundred thousand francs?

Rick

I appreciate it, but I don't accept it.

Laszlo

I'll raise it to two hundred thousand.

Rick

My friend, you could make it a million francs, or three; My answer would still be the same.

Laszlo

There must be some reason why you won't let me have them.

142

Rick
There is. I suggest that you ask your wife.

Laszlo looks at him, puzzled.

Laszlo
I beg your pardon?

Rick
I said, ask your wife.

Laszlo
My wife!

Rick
Yes.

Rick and Laszlo hear the sound of male voices singing downstairs. From the top of the stairs outside the office Rick sees a group of German officers around the piano singing the "Wacht am Rhein." Rick's expression is deadpan. Below, at the bar, Renault watches with raised eyebrow. Laszlo has come out of the office. His lips are very tight as he listens to the song. He starts down the steps, passes the table where Ilsa sits, and goes straight to the orchestra. Yvonne, sitting at a table with her German officer, stares down into her drink. Laszlo speaks to the orchestra.

Laszlo
Play the Marseillaise! Play it!

Members of the orchestra glance toward the steps, toward Rick, who nods to them. As they start to play, Laszlo and Carmina sing. Strasser conducts the German singing in an attempt to drown out the competition. People in the cafe begin to sing. Finally Strasser and his officers give up and sit down. The "Marseillaise" continues, however, and now Yvonne has jumped up and is singing with tears in her eyes. Ilsa, overcome with emotion, looks proudly at Laszlo who sings with passion. Finally the whole cafe is standing,

143

singing, their faces aglow. The song is finished on a high, triumphant note.

Yvonne's face is exalted. She deliberately faces the alcove where the Germans are watching. She shouts at the top of her lungs.

Yvonne
Vive La France! Vive la democracie!

Crowd
Vive La France! Vive la democracie!

People are clapping and cheering. Several French officers surround Laszlo, offering him a drink. Strasser's looks are not pleasant. He strides across the floor toward Renault who is standing at the bar.

Strasser
You see what I mean? If Laszlo's presence in a cafe can inspire this unfortunate demonstration, what more will his presence in Casablanca bring on? I advise that this place be shut up at once.

Renault
innocently
But everybody's having such a good time.

Strasser
Yes, much too good a time. The place is to be closed.

Renault
But I have no excuse to close it.

Strasser
snapping
Find one.

Renault thinks a moment, then blows a loud blast on his whistle. The room grows quiet, all eyes turn toward Renault.

144

Renault
loudly
Everybody is to leave here immediately! This cafe is closed until further notice!

An angry murmur starts among the crowd.

Renault
Clear the room at once!

Rick comes quickly up to Renault.

Rick
How can you close me up? On what grounds?

Renault
I am shocked, *shocked* to find that gambling is going on in here!

This display of nerve leaves Rick at a loss. The croupier comes out of the gambling room and up to Renault.

Croupier
handing Renault a roll of bills
Your winnings, sir.

Renault
Oh. Thank you very much.
turns to the crowd again
Everybody out at once!

As the cafe is emptying, Strasser approaches Ilsa. His manner is abrupt but cordial.

Strasser
Mademoiselle, after this disturbance it is not safe for Laszlo to stay in Casablanca.

Ilsa
This morning you implied it was not safe for him to leave Casablanca.

145

Strasser
That is also true, except for one destination, to return to occupied France.

Ilsa
Occupied France?

Strasser
Uh huh. Under a safe conduct from me.

Ilsa
with intensity
What value is that? You may recall what German guarantees have been worth in the past.

Strasser
There are only two other alternatives for him.

Ilsa
What are they?

Strasser
It is possible the French authorities will find a reason to put him in the concentration camp here.

Ilsa
And the other alternative?

Strasser
My dear Mademoiselle, perhaps you have already observed that in Casablanca, human life is cheap. Good night, Mademoiselle.

She looks at him, understanding what he means. He bows and exits as Laszlo arrives at the table. They start out of the cafe.

Ilsa
What happened with Rick?

Laszlo
We'll discuss it later.

146

In the hallway of the hotel, Ilsa and Laszlo are walking to their room. They enter. Laszlo switches on the light and walks to the window to draw the shade. Below, across the street, a man can be seen standing under an arch. Laszlo watches him.

Laszlo
as he draws the shade
Our faithful friend is still there.

Ilsa
Victor, please don't go to the underground meeting tonight.

Laszlo
soberly
I must.
adds, with a smile
Besides, it isn't often that a man has the chance to display heroics before his wife.

Ilsa
Don't joke. After Major Strasser's warning tonight, I am frightened.

Laszlo
To tell you the truth, I am frightened, too. Shall I remain here in our hotel room hiding, or shall I carry on the best I can?

Ilsa
Whatever I'd say, you'd carry on. Victor, why don't you tell me about Rick? What did you find out?

Laszlo
Apparently he has the letters.

Ilsa
Yes?

Laszlo

But no intention of selling them. One would think if sentiment wouldn't pe.suade him, money would.

Ilsa

ill at ease, trying to keep her voice steady
Did he give any reason?

Laszlo

He suggested I ask you.

Ilsa

Ask *me?*

Laszlo

Yes. He said, "Ask your wife." I don't know why he said that.

Ilsa walks to the bed and sits down. Laszlo turns off the light.

Laszlo

Well, our friend outside will think we've retired by now. I'll be going in a few minutes.

He sits down on the bed beside her. A silence falls between them. It grows strained. Finally,

Laszlo
quietly
Ilsa, I . . .

Ilsa
Yes?

A pause.

Laszlo

When I was in the concentration camp, were you lonely in Paris?

148

Their faces are barely visible in the darkness.

Ilsa
Yes, Victor, I was.

Laszlo
sympathetically
I know how it is to be lonely.
very quietly
Is there anything you wish to tell me?

Ilsa
she controls herself, speaking low
No, Victor, there isn't.

There is silence.

Laszlo
I love you very much, my dear.

Ilsa
barely able to speak
Yes. Yes, I know. Victor, whatever I do, will you believe
that I, that . . .

Laszlo
You don't even have to say it. I'll believe.

Bending down, he kisses her cheek.

Laszlo
getting up
Goodnight, dear.

Ilsa
Goodnight.
watching him go
Victor!

*She gets up and follows him to the door. He is just opening
it. In the slit of light from the hall, we see her face,
which is strained and worried. She hesitates.*

Ilsa
in a tone which suggests this is not what she had been tempted to say
Be careful.

Laszlo
Of course, I'll be careful.

He kisses her on the cheek and goes out the door. She stands there for a few seconds, then crosses to look out of the window. When she sees him walking down the street, she closes the blind again, gets a cloak from the bedroom and leaves.

Inside the cafe, Rick and Carl are bent over ledgers. Carl is very busy figuring.

Carl
looking up
Well, you are in pretty good shape, Herr Rick.

Rick
How long can I afford to stay closed?

Carl
Oh, two weeks, maybe three.

Rick
Maybe I won't have to. A bribe has worked before. In the meantime, everybody stays on salary.

Carl
Oh, thank you, Herr Rick. Sacha will be happy to hear it. I owe him money.

Rick
Now you finish locking up, will you, Carl?

Carl
I will. Then I am going to the meeting of the . . .

152

Rick
interrupting
Don't tell me where you're going.

Carl
with a smile
I won't.

Rick
Goodnight.

Carl
Goodnight, M'sieur Rick.

Rick walks up the stairs to his apartment. It is dark. When the door opens, light from the hall reveals a figure in the room. Rick lights a small lamp. There is Ilsa facing him, her face white but determined. Rick pauses for a moment in astonishment.

Rick
How did you get in?

Ilsa
The stairs from the street.

Rick
I told you this morning you'd come around, but this is a little ahead of schedule.
with mock politeness
Well, won't you sit down?

Ilsa
Richard, I had to see you.

Rick
You use "Richard" again? We're back in Paris.

Ilsa
Please.

153

Rick

Your unexpected visit isn't connected by any chance with the letters of transit? It seems as long as I have those letters I'll never be lonely.

Ilsa
looks at him directly
You can ask any price you want, but you must give me those letters.

Rick

I went all through that with your husband. It's no deal.

Ilsa

I know how you feel about me, but I'm asking you to put your feelings aside for something more important.

Rick

Do I have to hear again what a great man your husband is? What an important cause he's fighting for?

Ilsa

It was your cause, too. In your own way, you were fighting for the same thing.

Rick

I'm not fighting for anything anymore, except myself. I'm the only cause I'm interested in.

A pause. Ilsa deliberately takes a new approach.

Ilsa

Richard, Richard, we loved each other once. If those days meant anything at all to you . . .

Rick
harshly
I wouldn't bring up Paris if I were you. It's poor salesmanship.

154

Ilsa

Please. Please listen to me. If you knew what really happened, if you only knew the truth . . .

Rick

cuts in

I wouldn't believe you, no matter what you told me. You'd say anything now, to get what you want.

Ilsa

her temper flaring, scornful

You want to feel sorry for yourself, don't you? With so much at stake, all you can think of is your own feeling. One woman has hurt you, and you take your revenge on the rest of the world. You're a, you're a coward, and a weakling.

breaks

No. Oh, Richard, I'm sorry. I'm sorry, but, but you, you are our last hope. If you don't help us, Victor Laszlo will die in Casablanca.

Rick

What of it? I'm going to die in Casablanca. It's a good spot for it.

He turns away to light a cigarette.

Rick

turning back to Ilsa

Now, if you . . .

He stops short as he sees Ilsa. She is holding a small revolver in her hand.

Ilsa

All right. I tried to reason with you. I tried everything. Now I want those letters.

For a moment, a look of admiration comes into Rick's eyes.

Ilsa

Get them for me.

Rick

I don't have to. I got them right here.

Ilsa

Put them on the table.

Rick

shaking his head
No.

Ilsa

For the last time, put them on the table.

Rick

If Laszlo and the cause mean so much to you, you won't stop at anything. All right, I'll make it easier for you. Go ahead and shoot. You'll be doing me a favor.

Rick walks toward Ilsa. As he reaches her, her hand drops down.

Ilsa

almost hysterical
Richard, I tried to stay away. I thought I would never see you again, that you were out of my life.
walking to the window
The day you left Paris, if you knew what I went through! If you knew how much I loved you, how much I still love you!

Rick has taken Ilsa in his arms. He presses her tight to him and kisses her passionately. She is lost in his embrace.

Sometime later, Rick watches the revolving beacon light at the airport from his window. There is a bottle of champagne on the table and two half-filled glasses. Ilsa is talking. Rick is listening intently.

156

Rick
And then?

Ilsa
It wasn't long after we were married that Victor went back to Czechoslovakia. They needed him in Prague, but there the Gestapo were waiting for him. Just a two-line item in the paper: "Victor Laszlo apprehended. Sent to concentration camp." I was frantic. For months I tried to get word. Then it came. He was dead, shot trying to escape. I was lonely. I had nothing. Not even hope. Then I met you.

Rick
Why weren't you honest with me? Why did you keep your marriage a secret?

Ilsa
Oh, it wasn't my secret, Richard. Victor wanted it that way. Not even our closest friends knew about our marriage. That was his way of protecting me. I knew so much about his work, and if the Gestapo found out I was his wife it would be dangerous for me and for those working with us.

Rick
When did you first find out he was alive?

Ilsa
Just before you and I were to leave Paris together. A friend came and told me that Victor was alive. They were hiding him in a freight car on the outskirts of Paris. He was sick; he needed me. I wanted to tell you, but I, I didn't dare. I knew, I knew you wouldn't have left Paris, and the Gestapo would have caught you. So I . . . Well, well, you know the rest.

Rick
Huh. But it's still a story without an ending.
looks at her directly
What about now?

157

Ilsa
Now? I don't know.
simply
I know that I'll never have the strength to leave you again.

Rick
And Laszlo?

Ilsa
Oh, you'll help him now, Richard, won't you? You'll see that he gets out? Then he'll have his work, all that he's been living for.

Rick
All except one. He won't have you.

Ilsa
I can't fight it anymore. I ran away from you once. I can't do it again. Oh, I don't know what's right any longer. You'll have to think for both of us, for all of us.

Rick
All right, I will. Here's looking at you, kid.

Ilsa
I wish I didn't love you so much.

Laszlo and Carl are making their way through the darkness toward Rick's. The headlights of a speeding police car sweep toward them and they flatten themselves against a wall to avoid detection. The lights move past them.

Carl
I think we lost them.

Laszlo
Yes. I'm afraid they caught some of the others.

Carl
Come inside. Come.

158

Laszlo and Carl enter the cafe and cross toward the bar.

Carl
Come inside. I will help you. Come in here.

Laszlo
Thank you.

Carl
I will give you some water.

Inside the apartment, Rick and Ilsa hear voices below. Rick crosses to the door. Ilsa stands just in back of him. She makes a move as if to come out on the balcony but Rick's arm pushes her back. She withdraws behind the door as Rick walks out to the balcony railing.

Rick
Carl, what happened?

Both Carl and Laszlo look up.

Carl
excitedly
The police break up our meeting, Herr Rick! We escaped in the last moment.

Rick
Come up here a minute.

Carl looks up wonderingly, then starts toward the stairway.

Carl
Yes, I come.

Rick
I want you to turn out the light in the rear entrance. It might attract the police.

Carl
But Sacha always puts out that light . . .

159

Rick
cutting in
Tonight he forgot.

Carl
Yes, I come, I will do it.

At the top of the stairs, Carl sees Ilsa. He asks no questions.

Rick
in a low voice
I want you to take Miss Lund home.

Carl
Yes, sir.

As Carl goes through the door, Rick starts downstairs. Laszlo is wrapping one of the small bar towels around his cut wrist. Rick looks questioningly at the injured hand.

Laszlo
It's nothing. Just a little cut. We had to get through a window.

Rick walks to the bar, picks up a bottle, and pours a drink.

Rick
Well, this might come in handy.

Laszlo
Thank you.

Rick
Had a close one, eh?

Laszlo
Yes, rather.

Rick
Don't you sometimes wonder if it's worth all this? I mean what you're fighting for?

160

Laszlo

We might as well question why we breathe. If we stop breathing, we'll die. If we stop fighting our enemies, the world will die.

Rick

What of it? Then it'll be out of its misery.

Laszlo

You know how you sound, M'sieur Blaine? Like a man who's trying to convince himself of something he doesn't believe in his heart. Each of us has a destiny, for good or for evil.

Rick
dryly
Yes, I get the point.

Laszlo

I wonder if you do. I wonder if you know that you're trying to escape from yourself and that you'll never succeed.

Rick
ironically
You seem to know all about my "destiny."

Laszlo

I know a good deal more about you than you suspect. I know, for instance, that you are in love with a woman.
smiles just a little
It is perhaps a strange circumstance that we both should be in love with the same woman. The first evening I came here in this cafe, I knew there was something between you and Ilsa. Since no one is to blame, I, I demand no explanation. I ask only one thing. You won't give me the letters of transit. All right. But I want my wife to be safe. I ask you as a favor to use the letters to take her away from Casablanca.

Rick looks at Laszlo incredulously.

Rick
You love her that much?

Laszlo
Apparently you think of me only as the leader of a cause.
Well, I am also a human being.
looks away for a moment, then quietly
Yes, I love her that much.

*At this moment there is a crashing sound at the door of the
cafe, followed by the forced entry of several gendarmes. A
French officer walks into the lighted area and addresses
Laszlo.*

French Officer
Mr. Laszlo?

Laszlo
Yes?

French Officer
You will come with us. We have a warrant for your arrest.

Laszlo
On what charge?

French Officer
Captain Renault will discuss that with you later.

Rick
smiles ironically
It seems that "destiny" has taken a hand.

*Laszlo looks for a moment at Rick, then in dignified silence
crosses to the officer. Together they walk toward the door.
Rick's eyes follow them, but his expression reveals nothing
of his feelings.*

The next morning in Renault's office. Rick is there.

162

Rick

But you haven't any actual proof, and you know it. This isn't Germany or occupied France. All you can do is fine him a few thousand francs and give him thirty days. You might as well let him go now.

Renault

Ricky, I'd advise you not to be too interested in what happens to Laszlo. If by any chance you were to help him to escape . . .

Rick

cutting in
What makes you think I'd stick my neck out for Laszlo?

Renault

Because, one, you have bet ten thousand francs he'd escape. Two, you have the letters of transit, now don't bother to deny it. And, well, you might do it simply because you don't like Strasser's looks. As a matter of fact, I don't like him either.

Rick

Well, they're all excellent reasons.

Renault

Don't count too much on my friendship, Ricky. In this matter I'm powerless. Besides, I might lose the ten thousand francs.

Rick

You're not very subtle, but you are effective. I, I get the point. Yes, I have the letters, but I intend using them myself. I'm leaving Casablanca on tonight's plane, the last plane.

Renault
Huh?

Rick
And I'm taking a friend with me.

163

smiles
One you'll appreciate.

Renault
What friend?

Rick
Ilsa Lund.

An amazed incredulity is written on Renault's face.

Rick
That ought to put your mind to rest about my helping Laszlo escape. The last man I want to see in America.

Renault
shrewdly
You didn't come here to tell me this. You have the letters of transit. You can fill in your name and hers and leave any time you please. Why are you still interested in what happens to Laszlo?

Rick
I'm not. But I *am* interested in what happens to Ilsa and me. We have a legal right to go, that's true. But people have been held in Casablanca in spite of their legal rights.

Renault
What makes you think we want to hold you?

Rick
Ilsa is Laszlo's wife. She probably knows things that Strasser would like to know. Louis, I'll make a deal with you. Instead of this petty charge you have against him, you can get something really big, something that would chuck him in a concentration camp for years. That would be quite a feather in your cap, wouldn't it?

Renault
It certainly would. Germany . . .
corrects himself
Vichy would be very grateful.
164

Rick

Then release him. You be at my place a half an hour before the plane leaves. I'll arrange to have Laszlo come there to pick up the letters of transit, and that'll give you the criminal grounds on which to make the arrest. You get him, and we get away. To the Germans that last will be just a minor annoyance.

Renault
puzzled
There's still something about this business I don't quite understand. Miss Lund, she's very beautiful, yes, but you were never interested in any woman.

Rick

Well, she isn't just any woman.

Renault

I see. How do I know you'll keep your end of the bargain?

Rick

I'll make the arrangements right now with Laszlo in the visitor's pen.

Renault

Ricky, I'm going to miss you. Apparently you're the only one in Casablanca who has even less scruples than I.

Rick
dryly
Oh, thanks.

Renault

Go ahead, Ricky.

Rick

And by the way, call off your watchdogs when you let him go. I don't want them around this afternoon. I'm taking no chances, Louis, not even with you.

A waiter at the Blue Parrot is bringing coffee into Ferrari's office. Rick and Ferrari are sitting there.

Ferrari

Shall we draw up papers, or is our handshake good enough?

Rick

It's certainly not good enough. But since I'm in a hurry, it'll have to do.

Ferrari

Oh, to get out of Casablanca and go to America! You're a lucky man.

Rick

Oh, by the way, my agreement with Sam's always been that he gets twenty-five percent of the profits. That still goes.

Ferrari

Hm. I happen to know he gets ten percent. But he's worth twenty-five.

Rick

And Abdul and Carl and Sacha, they stay with the place, or I don't sell.

Ferrari

Of course they stay. Rick's wouldn't be Rick's without them.

Rick

getting up
Well, so long.
he walks to the door, stops, turns
Don't forget, you owe Rick's a hundred cartons of American cigarettes.

Ferrari

I shall remember to pay it to myself.

Rick leaves. Ferrari swats a fly on the table.

166

Outside Rick's Cafe, a huge placard is pasted on the door:
CLOSED
By Order of the Prefect of Police
Someone knocks on the door. Rick is seated at a table inside reading the letters of transit. When he hears the knock, he puts them away in his pocket and goes to the door. It is Renault.
Rick
You're late.
Renault
I was informed just as Laszlo was about to leave the hotel, so I knew I would be on time.
Rick
I thought I asked you to tie up your watch-dogs.
Renault
Oh, he won't be followed here.
looks around the empty cafe
You know, this place will never be the same without you, Ricky.
Rick
Yes, I know what you mean, but I've already spoken to Ferrari. You'll still win at roulette.
Renault
Is everything ready?
Rick
tapping his breast pocket
I have the letters right here.
Renault
Tell me, when we searched the place, where were they?
Rick
Sam's piano.
Renault
Serves me right for not being musical!
The sound of a car pulling up is heard.
Rick
Oh. Here they are. You'd better wait in my office.
Renault walks up to the office. Outside, Laszlo is paying the cabdriver. Ilsa is walking toward the entrance.
Laszlo
to the cabdriver
Here.

Inside, Rick opens the door. Ilsa rushes in. Her intensity reveals the strain she is under.

Ilsa
Richard, Victor thinks I'm leaving with him. Haven't you told him?

Rick
No, not yet.

Ilsa
But it's all right, isn't it? You were able to arrange everything?

Rick
Everything is quite all right.

Ilsa
Oh, Rick!
She looks at him with a vaguely questioning look.

Rick
We'll tell him at the airport. The less time to think, the easier for all of us. Please trust me.

Ilsa
Yes, I will.

Laszlo comes in.

Laszlo
M'sieur Blaine. I don't know how to thank you.

Rick
Oh, save it. We've still lots of thinks to do.

Laszlo
I brought the money, M'sieur Blaine.

Rick
Keep it. You'll need it in America.

Laszlo
But we made a deal.

Rick
cutting him short
Oh, never mind about that. You won't have any trouble in Lisbon, will you?

Laszlo
No. It's all arranged.

170

Rick

Good. I've got the letters right here, all made out in blank.

takes out the letters

All you have to do is fill in the signatures.

He hands them to Laszlo, who takes them gratefully.

Renault's Voice

Victor Laszlo!

Renault is at the bottom of the stairs.

Renault

Victor Laszlo, you are under arrest on a charge of accessory to the murder of the couriers from whom these letters were stolen.

Ilsa and Laszlo are both caught completely off guard. They turn toward Rick. Horror is in Ilsa's eyes. Renault takes the letters.

Renault

Oh, you are surprised about my friend, Ricky? The explanation is quite simple. Love, it seems, has triumphed over virtue. Thank . . .

Obviously, the situation delights Renault. He is smiling as he turns toward Rick. Suddenly the smile fades. In Rick's hand is a gun which he is leveling at Renault.

Rick

Not so fast, Louis. Nobody's going to be arrested. Not for a while yet.

Renault

Have you taken leave of your senses?

Rick

I have. Sit down over there.

Renault hesitates, then walks toward Rick.

Renault

Put that gun down.

Rick

putting his hand up to stop Renault

Louis, I wouldn't like to shoot you, but I will, if you take one more step.

Renault halts for a moment and studies Rick.

Renault
Under the circumstances, I will sit down.

He walks to a table and sits down.

Rick
sharply
Keep your hands on the table.

Renault
I suppose you know what you're doing, but I wonder if you realize what this means?

Rick
I do. We've got plenty of time to discuss that later.

Renault
reproachfully, to Rick
"Call off your watch-dogs," you said.

Rick
Just the same, you call the airport and let me hear you tell them. And remember, this gun's pointed right at your heart.

Renault
as he dials
That is my least vulnerable spot.

Rick takes back the letters.

Renault
into the phone
Hello, is that the airport? This is Captain Renault speaking. There'll be two letters of transit for the Lisbon plane. There's to be not trouble about them. Good.

In the German consulate, Strasser is jiggling the telephone receiver violently.

Strasser
Hello? Hello?
He hangs up the receiver momentarily, presses a buzzer on his desk, then again lifts the receiver.

Strasser
to an officer entering
My car, quickly!

172

Officer

Zu Befehl, Herr Major.

The officer exits and Strasser resumes on the telephone.

Strasser

This is Major Strasser. Have a squad of police meet me at the airport at once. At once! Do you hear?

Hanging up the receiver, and grabbing his cap, he hurriedly exits.

At the airport, the outline of the transport plane is barely visible. A uniformed orderly is at the telephone near the hangar door.

Orderly

Hello. Hello, radio tower? Lisbon plane taking off in ten minutes. East runway. Visibility: one and a half miles. Light ground fog. Depth of fog: approximately 500. Ceiling: unlimited. Thank you.

He hangs up, and crosses to the car that has just pulled up. Renault gets out, closely followed by Rick, hand in pocket, still covering Renault with a gun. Laszlo and Ilsa come from the rear of the car.

Rick

indicating the orderly

Louis, have your man go with Mr. Laszlo and take care of his luggage.

Renault

bows ironically

Certainly Rick. Anything you say.

to orderly

Find Mr. Laszlo's luggage and put it on the plane.

Orderly

Yes, sir. This way please.

The orderly escorts Laszlo off in the direction of the plane. Rick takes the letters of transit out of his pocket, and hands them to Renault.

Rick

If you don't mind, you fill in the names.

smiles

That will make it even more official.

Renault
You think of everything, don't you?

Rick
quietly
And the names are Mr. and Mrs. Victor Laszlo.

Both Ilsa and Renault look at Rick with astonishment.

Ilsa
But why *my* name, Richard?

Rick
watching Renault
Because you're getting on that plane.

Ilsa
dazed
I don't understand. What about you?

Rick
I'm staying here with him 'til the plane gets safely away.

Ilsa
as Rick's intention fully dawns on her
No, Richard, no. What has happened to you? Last night we said . . .

Rick
Last night we said a great many things. You said I was to do he thinking for both of us. Well, I've done a lot of it since then and it all adds up to one thing. You're getting on that plane with Victor where you belong.

Ilsa
protesting
But Richard, no, I, I . . .

Rick
Now you've got to listen to me. Do you have any idea what you'd have to look forward to if you stayed here? Nine chances out of ten we'd both wind up in a concentration camp. Isn't that true, Louis?

Renault
as he countersigns the papers
I am afraid that Major Strasser would insist.

174

Ilsa

turns to Rick

You're saying this only to make me go.

Rick

I'm saying it because it's true. Inside of us we both know you belong with Victor. You're part of his work, the thing that keeps him going. If that plane leaves the ground and you're not with him, you'll regret it.

Ilsa

No.

Rick

Maybe not today, maybe not tomorrow, but soon, and for the rest of your life.

Ilsa

But what about us?

Rick

We'll always have Paris. We didn't have it, we'd lost it, until you came to Casablanca. We got it back last night .

Ilsa

And I said I would never leave you!

Rick

And you never will. But I've got a job to do, too. Where I'm going you can't follow. What I've got to do, you can't be any part of. Ilsa, I'm no good at being noble, but it doesn't take much to see that the problems of three little people don't amount to a hill of beans in this crazy world. Someday you'll understand that. Not now. Here's looking at you, kid.

At this moment, Laszlo comes back.

Laszlo

Everything is in order?

Rick

All except one thing. There's something you should know before you leave.

Laszlo

sensing what is coming

Monsieur Blaine, I don't ask you to explain anything.

Rick

I'm going to anyway, because it may make a difference to you later on. You said you knew about Ilsa and me.

Laszlo

Yes.

Rick

But you didn't know she was at my place last night when you were. She came there for the letters of transit. Isn't that true, Ilsa?

Ilsa

facing Laszlo
Yes.

Rick

his voice more harsh, almost brutal
She tried everything to get them, and nothing worked. She did her best to convince me that she was still in love with me, but that was all over long ago. For your sake, she pretended it wasn't, and I let her pretend.

Laszlo

I understand.
Rick hands him the letters.

Rick

Here it is.

Laszlo

Thanks. I appreciate it. And welcome back to the fight. This time I know our side wil win.
On the field, the airplane propellers start turning.

Laszlo

Are you ready, Ilsa?

Ilsa looks at Rick for the last time.

Ilsa

Yes, I'm ready.
to Rick
Goodbye, Rick. God bless you.

Rick

You better hurry, or you'll miss that plane.

As Ilsa and Laszlo leave in the direction of the plane, Renault regards Rick triumphantly.

176

Renault

Well, I was right! You *are* a sentimentalist!

Rick

Stay where you are! I don't know what you're talking about.

Renault

What you just did for Laszlo, and that fairy tale you invented to send Ilsa away with him. I know a little about women, my friend. She went, but she knew you were lying.

Rick

Anyway, thanks for helping me out.

Rick's face reveals nothing.

Renault

I suppose you know this isn't going to be very pleasant for either of us, especially for you. I'll have to arrest you, of course.

Rick

As soon as the plane goes, Louis.

As the door to the plane is finally closed, Strasser's car screeches to a halt in front of the hangar. Strasser jumps out of the car and runs toward Renault.

Strasser

What was the meaning of that phone call?

Renault

Victor Laszlo is on that plane.

He nods off down the field. Strasser turns to see the plane taxiing toward the runway.

Strasser

Why do you stand here? Why don't you stop him?

Renault
Ask M'sieur Rick.

Strasser looks briefly at Rick, then makes a step toward the telephone just inside the hangar door. Rick points the revolver at Strasser.

Rick
Get away from that phone!

Strasser stops in his tracks, looks at Rick, and sees that he means business.

Strasser
steely
I would advise you not to interfere.

Rick
I was willing to shoot Captain Renault, and I'm willing to shoot you.

Strasser runs toward the telephone. He desperately grabs the receiver.

Strasser
into phone
Hello?

Rick
Put that phone down!

Strasser
Get me the Radio Tower!

Rick
Put it down!

Strasser, his one hand holding the receiver, pulls out a pistol with the other hand and shoots quickly at Rick. The bullet misses, but Rick's shot has hit Strasser, who crumples to the ground.

180

A police car speeds up to the hangar. Four gendarmes jump out. In the distance, the plane is turning onto the runway. The gendarmes run to Renault. Renault turns to them.

Gendarme
Mon Capitaine!

Renault
Major Strasser's been shot.
pauses as he looks at Rick, then to the gendarmes
Round up the usual suspects.

Gendarme
Oui, mon Capitaine.

He leads the other gendarmes off. The two men look at one another. Renault picks up a bottle of Vichy water and opens it.

Renault
Well, Rick, you're not only a sentimentalist, but you've become a patriot.

Rick
Maybe, but it seemed like a good time to start.

Renault
I think perhaps you're right.

As he pours the water into a glass, Renault sees the Vichy label and quickly drops the bottle into a trash basket which he then kicks over.

Rick and Renault watch the plane take off, maintaining their gaze until it disappears into the clouds.

Renault
It might be a good idea for you to disappear from Casablanca for a while. There's a Free French garrison over at Brazzaville. I could be induced to arrange a passage.

181

Rick
smiles
My letter of transit? I could use a trip. But it doesn't make any difference about our bet. You still owe me ten thousand francs.

Renault
And that ten thousand francs should pay our expenses.

Rick
Our expenses!

Renault
Uh huh.

Rick
Louis, I think this is the beginning of a beautiful friendship.

Rick and Renault walk off together into the night.

THE END

Richard Corliss

ANALYSIS OF THE FILM

When *Casablanca* first appeared, toward the end of 1942, few movie-wise people would have bet that screen history was about to be embossed on the Warner Brothers shield. Hal Wallis had a topical subject on which to base another hit production—but everybody was making war-effort movies. Moreover, the final script—which bore some unrecognizable traces of *Everybody Comes to Rick's,* "one of the world's worst plays" according to James Agee—had been written at breakneck speed and under appalling pressure by a junior member of the Warners writing pool, Howard Koch, after the studio's prolific Epstein brothers had made their contributions and had moved on to another, presumably more important assignment.

Although *Casablanca* defines Bogie for all time as the existential-hero-in-spite-of-himself, several of his roles just preceding this one (notably *High Sierra* and *The Maltese Falcon*) had prepared his fans for the misanthropy and climactic selflessness he would embody as Rick Blaine. Bergman (as Ilsa Lund) and Henreid (as Victor Laszlo) are hardly incandescent lovers—neither are Bergman and Bogart, for that matter—but their very turgidity as sexual partners works, intentionally or not, to the film's advantage. Claude Rains had played a perplexing variety of roles: some sympathetic (*Now, Voyager*), some unsympathetic (*Crime Without Passion*), and some in which he was a good man weak enough to fall prey to overwhelming forces (scientific megalomania in *The Invisible Man,* political corruption in *Mr. Smith Goes to Washington*); audiences weren't sure of the proper moral attitude to assume toward Rains, and this made him perfect for the suave, enigmatic Louis Renault. The outrageously dense supporting cast of Conrad Veidt, Peter Lorre, Sidney Greenstreet, Dooley Wilson, S. Z. Sakall, Leonid Kinskey, John Qualen, Curt Bois, Marcel Dalio, and dozens of others would have lent a certain spurious sense of resonance to *A History of the*

Blue Movie, let alone to a film in which each player is adroitly cast and allowed a privileged moment or two all his own. Michael Curtiz had directed forty-two films in the previous decade for Warners and, when one considers the restrictions on shot-planning and script-doctoring inherent in such a prodigious output, the generally high quality of his work is impressive. Undoubtedly, much of the film's verve and terse efficiency—as well as its occasionally hurried, perfunctory *mise-en-scène*—can be traced to Curtiz.

But the success of *Casablanca* ultimately derives from the character development and dialogue. Warners would again assemble attractive casts, and assign Curtiz to direct them—as with *Passage to Marseilles.* None of the sequels was as richly textured, as effortlessly witty, as complex in characterization, as entertaining or, consequently, as popular as *Casablanca.* On the other hand, when Koch had the opportunity, five years later, to work with Max Ophuls on *Letter from an Unknown Woman,* he produced a script as drenched in delicate Viennese irony as *Casablanca* was suffused with the more pungent irony of an occupied city where all roles are uncertain, and thus played to the hilt— and where the only values are the shifting ones of the Vichy franc, and thus gambled on with a desperation that tries to pass for insouciance.

I

The vigorous stoicism with which Rick Blaine surrenders Ilsa to Laszlo, and the pleasure he exudes in walking with Renault into the final fade-out, have given rise to two seductive theories about the film, one pertinent and one impertinent. The first is that *Casablanca* is a political allegory, with Rick as President Roosevelt (*casa blanca* is Spanish for "white house"), a man who gambles on the odds of going to war until circumstance and his own submerged nobility force him to close his casino (read: partisan politics) and commit himself—first by financing the Side of Right and then by fighting for it. The time of the film's action (December, 1941) adds credence to this

186

view, as does the irrelevant fact that, two months after *Casablanca* opened, Roosevelt (Rick) and Prime Minister Winston Churchill (Laszlo) met for a war conference in Casablanca.

The other theory proposes *Casablanca* as a repressed homosexual fantasy, in which Rick rejects his token mistress for an honest if furtive affair with another man. Now, Rick is hardly "rough trade," and Renault's exhaustive string of conquests attests to his performance, if not his preference. Still, they make an intriguing active-passive pair. Renault flirts with Rick—indeed, he flirts with everyone—throughout the film, and at one point he tells Ilsa, "He is the kind of man that . . . well, if I were a woman, and *I* were not around, I should be in love with Rick." The pansexual sophistication of the Seventies makes such inferences as these appealing, especially when we can attach them to artifacts from our own primitive past. But we should be careful when we paint yesterday's picture in today's colors; tomorrow they may seem gaudily inappropriate. At the time Renault speaks to Ilsa, he doesn't know that she was and is "in love with Rick." Ilsa, however, loves an idealized Rick—a socialist adventurer, who fought on the right sides in Ethiopia and Spain—while Renault loves or likes or admires the real Rick, who uses his financial and sexual authority to throw Nazis out of his cafe and idealists out of his life (the latter more gently, to be sure). For Rick, women are an occasional obsession; for Renault they are a perpetual diversion. Both want companionship more than they need love. If audiences did not intuit this preference, they wouldn't accept the film's ending with such supreme satisfaction.

Besides, Renault's presumed ambisexuality is of less interest than his genuine ambiguity. When Renault's tongue is not in his cheek (a place of relative repose), it is darting out to catch the weary or unwary females who buzz into Casablanca hoping for a visa. Renault is not rapacious so much as he is pleased by the power that he wields and amused at the indignities men must endure—and women must enjoy—for him to use that power to their benefit. He is radiantly corrupt. He has style. What Rick thinks of, early in the film, as political realism, Renault knows is expediency. In Rick, American pragmatism has soured into phlegmatism, while in Renault, French charm has degenerated into coquetry. But Rick can give Renault a sense of values, and Renault can give Rick a sense of proportion; both have a sardonic sense of humor. In Jungian terms, Rick is the *animus* of this split personality and Renault is the *anima*. Or, as they used to say at Schwabb's, the two are made for each other.

Rick and Renault share the economic and spiritual leadership of Vichy-ruled Casablanca with Signor Ferrari (Sidney Greenstreet), the black-market boss who can say simply, "As leader of all illegal activities in Casablanca, I am an influential and respected man." This odd troika presides over a populace that is either flourishing or desperate, depending on their ability to hustle persuasively, and regardless of their former status. Thus, a beautiful woman tells her companion, an old letch: "It used to take a villa at Cannes, or the very least, a string of pearls. Now all I ask is an exit visa." (Her plight was even more serious than she had feared: her dialogue was cut from the completed film.) When the manager of "the second largest banking house in Amsterdam" tries to bribe Carl, the headwaiter, for a drink with Rick, Carl replies that "the leading banker is the pastry chef in our kitchen," and pockets the money. Carl, whom the script describes as the author of books on "mathematics . . . astronomy . . . the greatest professor in the whole University of Leipzig," represents the humanistic—that is, the Jewish—side of the German psyche.

Of Rick's other employees, the bartender (Leonid Kinskey) had been "the Czar's favorite sword-swallower"; Abdul the doorman (Dan Seymour) adds some local color to the café, if not to the film; and the croupier of Rick's illegal gambling table is given no specific past, but since he is played by Marcel Dalio, reverberations of his tainted aristocracy in *The Rules of the Game* may appear on the seismographic memories of some moviegoers. The only member of Rick's retinue who indicates any integrity with his own past is Sam, the piano player (Dooley Wilson), who had been Rick's companion four years earlier in Paris—when Rick and Ilsa fell in love—and shares the

188

same relationship with him in Casablanca. The continuity of Sam's function suggests that the light-hearted Rick of Paris and the pessimistic Rick of Casablanca are closer to one another than his crude bitterness toward Ilsa later on in the café would imply. At any rate, Rick's role to the rest of his staff is that of the curt if protective patriarch, whereas he shows Sam a courtesy that he reveals to few others, usually prefacing requests with a gentlemanly "do you mind." Indeed, Ferrari's offer to "buy" Sam, along with Rick's saloon, drives Rick to a rare flight of self-righteousness—"I don't buy or sell human beings"—which leads us to believe that, at this point in the film at least, Sam is one of the few beings in Casablanca whom Rick would consider human.

II

After a brief montage of animated maps describing the European emigré's route through Casablanca, the film's irony and the city's duplicity are immediately established with the entrance of the Dark European (Curt Bois). The term is both literal and metaphorical: this guy is doubly shady, pursuing the pickpocket's profession by warning his suckers, with a great show of concern, about the many pickpockets in town. With a pithiness typical of both the characters and the dialogue, the writers not only establish the sinister dexterity of this Dark European—and, by extension, of all those who flourish in Casablanca—but also impart some crucial plot information. "Two German couriers were found murdered in the desert. (*With an ironic smile* [says the script]) The . . . unoccupied desert." They had been carrying letters of transit—visas which cannot be questioned—papers whose fateful power will bring all who touch them close to death, like the sexual love that turns to syphilis in Schnitzler's *La Ronde*.

The sign by the door of Captain Renault's *Palais de Justice*—itself an ironic title—reads *"Liberté, Egalité, Fraternité."* The film will place a fairly grave accent on Liberty (as personified by Ilsa and Laszlo) and a cute accent on Fraternity (as exemplified by Rick and Renault).

189

As for equality . . . well, this is an African country run by white Europeans; there is a Dark European in the film, but no blackamoor. Economic and sexual equality are also ignored. In the words of the Dark European, "The rich and beautiful sail to Lisbon. The poor are always with us."

Even Major Strasser (Conrad Veidt), Laszlo's formidable pursuer and the chief representative of the Third Reich's arrogance and humorlessness, is entertaining in a verminous way—a quality that would be lacking in later Hollywood Nazis, once the makers of war movies decided that putting a two- or three-dimensional villain on the screen was a creative act of treason. Strasser can't help but be affected by the irony that laces Casablanca's humid air, and he occasionally jousts with Renault and, later, with Rick and Laszlo. But he always loses in these contests of wit, if only because of his grim, heavy-handed determination to win.

Whenever a long-lost love emerges from the machine-made mists of a Hollywood hero's past, an "other woman" is needed to add a little dramatic tension to the confrontation in the present. Rick's present is clouded by such a smoke-screen of cynicism that an alluring third party would be redundant—but one is provided anyway: Yvonne. Her main function, aside from ever-so-tenuously indicating Rick's vacillation between German power and Allied positive thinking, is to act as foil for two of *Casablanca*'s most quoted lines. More than any other, this bit of dialogue established Rick and Bogart as early existential heroes.

YVONNE: Where were you last night?
RICK: That's so long ago, I don't remember.
YVONNE (*after a pause*): Will I see you tonight?
RICK: I never make plans that far ahead.

With the merest suggestion that his stoic rejection of Yvonne will save her a lot of heartache (and save him a few annoying hysteria scenes), Rick sends her home—with Sacha, who really loves her. Rick seems to throw away women with the same assured carelessness he evinces in throwing away lines; but there is hardly ever a wasted motion in either his actions or his dialogue. Here he has obliquely stated his philosophy, ended a tedious affair, and made a match. He has also lured Renault into the conversation, for the Captain, after chiding Rick on his extravagance with women (Rains says, "Someday they may be scarce," but the original line is wittier and more relevant: "Someday they may be rationed"), allows that he is interested in Yvonne himself. Rick, it would seem, can have any woman he wants—and yet he doesn't seem to want any.

> RENAULT: I have often speculated on why you don't return to America. Did you abscond with the church funds? Did you run off with a Senator's wife? I like to think you killed a man. It is the romantic in me.
> RICK (*sardonically*): It was a combination of all three.

For some, Casablanca is a purgatory where their worldly sins—money, jewels, political connections—must be bartered away in order to get out. For others—the omnipresent but unseen poor—Casablanca is sheer hell, with no hope of redemption. For Rick it is Limbo, a state of suspended spiritual animation. We never do find out about Rick's distant past, although he finds out about Ilsa's; perhaps this is one reason why the Bogart character lives today, while Bergman's Ilsa has lost co-starred billing in the minds of *Casablanca*'s devotees to Rick's partner in enigmatic ambiguity, Louis Renault. But while Rick's sardonic evasion doesn't tell us about his past, it does portend future events which only he can control. The film's climax will have Rick "abscond with the church funds" by selling his saloon to Ferrari, "run off with a Senator's wife" by leaving Casablanca in the company of the coquettish representative from Vichy, and "kill a man"—Major Strasser.

> RENAULT: And what in heaven's name brought you to Casablanca?
> RICK: My health. I came to Casablanca for the waters.
> RENAULT: Waters? What waters? We're in the desert.

RICK: I was misinformed.

The Pinteresque understatement of Rick's ludicrous "explanation" telegraphs to Renault elements of pastness that point to his reluctance to explain himself. And yet there is some truth in his nimble evasion, as we will discover. Some years before, Rick was "misinformed." *That* sent him away from Paris, and eventually brought him to Casablanca.

Rick is even nimbler, and more oblique, about his dormant political nobility. We know he ran guns to Ethiopia in 1935, and fought for the Loyalists in 1936, long-shot activities that make his current political and sexual neutrality look more counter-revolutionary than it would otherwise. But when Strasser tries to intimidate Rick by reading him a Nazi-researched dossier of these adventures, Rick simply glances at the German's little black book and, with a bland expression that perfectly reveals his contempt for the obviousness of Strasser's methods, asks, "Are my eyes really brown?" This blending of the modest and the arrogant, the casual and the ballsy, stamps Rick as a man of courage as indelibly as will his climactic heroism. For here he has nothing to gain by his bravado except an affirmation of his self-respect—and an off-hand solicitation of Renault's respect, which one doubts Rick values very highly. Nevertheless, when Renault (in the same conversation) says of Laszlo, "Of course, one must admit he has great courage," it is a tribute that Rick has already earned for himself.

Laszlo *is* courageous. True, the oratorical skills necessary in a Resistance leader—not to mention his lame-duck role in the plot—frequently draw him into pomposity and self-righteousness. But Laszlo can be ironic when irony is needed, if only to Advance The Cause. (Humorless men, like Laszlo, like Strasser, indeed like Charles Foster Kane, can use humor to their advantage: to convert, to threaten, to *seem* human. These three men, superficially so different, are tied together by their use of power and people. They are all public men; only their goals distinguish them.) Thus, when an underground contact (John Qualen) tells Laszlo that he has "read five times that you were killed in five different places," Laszlo replies, *(smiling wryly)* "As you can see, it was true every single time." In fact, the life of a fugitive has sapped enough of Laszlo's strength so that he must channel all of it into politics, and too little of it to his love, his wife, Ilsa.

Four years earlier, in pre-Occupation Paris, Ilsa had been only a mystery woman ("I know so little about you—just the fact that you had your teeth straightened"). Now, in Casablanca, she is a phantom. Once she had been the repository of Rick's romantic love and political idealism, to such an extent that distinctions between personal obsessions and political affections blurred and then merged. When the Nazis moved into Paris, she moved out of his life; Rick's idealism and love, because they had become inseparable, were fatally dissolved on the same day. The death of romance left a rancid crust of cynicism upon Rick's soul, and over the years the crust hardened to form a casket for his optimism and nobility. The crucial dramatic question is whether her reappearance after such a long time—a lifetime, a death time—will help revive that Parisian optimism or bury it for good; and whether, once Ilsa has resurrected Rick's romantic love and political idealism, he will be able to suppress the former for the sake of the latter.

In the 1937 flashback, Rick bombards Ilsa with the kind of questions his Casablanca acquaintances would later ask him: "Who are you really, and what were you before? What did you do, and what did you think?" His famous toast—"Here's looking at you, kid"—can be read as meaning, "Here's trying to look into your soul, kid, to figure out who you really are." For most of *Casablanca,* Rick and Ilsa and Laszlo are defined not only by their pasts but by the suspicions other characters have about these pasts. Ilsa in 1937 and Rick in 1941 are evasive for the same reason: for each, a love affair melded into international affairs so imperceptibly and so relentlessly that telling one's confession would sound like a chaotic, personalized history lesson. The film's *denouement* will, for Rick, be literally that—an "unraveling" of future conditional from past imperfect, of Western Civilization from autobiography, of duty from love.

193

Ilsa is basically a simple country girl; *her* irony is platitudinous. "With the whole world crumbling, we pick this time to fall in love," she says to Rick in Paris (it will be as appropriate in Casablanca). And "Was that cannon fire, or was it the pounding of my heart?" Ilsa is the sort of serious, naïve young woman who would express the most exalted of emotions in the rhetoric of a Hollywood love story—unlike Rick and Renault, whose diction and delivery indicate a more genuine, more assured compatibility.

As signposts to the film's plot and characterization, these lines have meanings they lack as stabs at rapier wit. When Ilsa dodges Rick's probes into her past and his demands on her future (even saying, in response to Rick's suggestion that they get married as soon as they arrive in Marseilles, that "That's too far ahead to plan"), she is unknowingly clarifying Rick's abrupt dismissal of Yvonne: Rick's quest for a past and hope for a future with Ilsa had inflamed a love that disappointment turned to ashes—"once burned, twice shy." When she tells Rick that "you must leave Paris" and he replies, "No, *we* must leave," Ilsa is preparing the viewer for Rick's final choice of the greatest good for the greatest number over an easy solution to "the problems of three little people."

Of course, Rick leaves Paris alone, with the Paris rain smudging Ilsa's farewell letter as a considerate substitute for Rick's (and Bogart's) reluctant tears. The flashback ends with drunkenly bleary instead of heroically teary—the cynic's attempt to becloud pain with a dull gauze rather than letting it all drip out. When Ilsa interrupts Rick's masochistic reverie to tell him about her marriage to Laszlo then and now, Rick accuses her of literal and political prostitution—the loser's attempt to punish himself by hurting someone he may still love. As Ilsa walks out, Rick surrenders to one of those rare waste motions that reveal the unwinding of his coiled composure: he collapses, heart-broken and instantly hung-over, like the sort of drunk "M'sieur Rick" would throw out of his cafe without breaking his stride, his composure, or the silky pattern of his dialogue.

194

III

The galaxy of supporting characters in *Casablanca* constitute a dazzling, baroque hall of mirrors that reflect facets and distortions of the leading characters' lives and life-styles. Ugarte and Ferrari are various corruptions of Rick, as peddler and panderer, respectively; Carl is a cuddly, less ostentatious Laszlo; Sacha is an unseductive Renault; Yvonne and the Dark European share Rick's indecision between Free France and the Third Reich; Strasser is a German version of Renault, a prosaic scientist of war to Renault's master of the boudoir arts, the crazy-mirror image of an *übermensch* as opposed to Renault's *homme moyen sensuel.* The film is almost symphonic in the way its reflections of plot and reverberations of dialogue help to reinforce themes and deepen our understanding of Rick and Renault, Ilsa and Laszlo. One of these variations which almost amounts to a subplot, involves Rick and Annina, a young Bulgarian woman determined to get herself and her calf-like husband to America—even if it means meeting Captain Renault's stiff price. Annina's plea to Rick for advice is practically a *précis* of the film's dilemma.

> ANNINA: M'sieur, you are a man. If someone loved you very much, so that your happiness was the only thing that she wanted in the whole world but she did a bad thing to make certain of it, could you forgive her?
> RICK: Nobody ever loved me that much.
> ANNINA: And he never knew and the girl kept this bad thing locked in her heart? That would be all right, wouldn't it?
> RICK *(harshly)*: You want my advice?
> ANNINA: Oh, yes, please.
> RICK: Go back to Bulgaria.

There's nothing neat about the analogy of subplot to plot here. What is clear is that the Rick-Annina dialogue acts both as echo and as presentiment. Annina's forthrightness and bravery, as much as anything else, convince Rick that he should revise his estimation of Ilsa's attachment for him; perhaps, at the moment he mutters "nobody ever loved me that much," Rick realizes how much Ilsa loved and admired him—enough to believe he had the strength to survive a bitterly cruel disillusionment. Rick "never knew"; Ilsa "kept this bad thing locked in her heart"; and ultimately she "went back" to Czechoslovakia in the person of Victor Laszlo. Of course, Ilsa didn't guarantee Rick's (or Laszlo's) happiness by leaving him to join Laszlo. And, when she comes to his apartment later to get the letters of transit, it won't be because she loves Laszlo "very much," at least not romantically, or even personally: only as the embodiment of a great cause. Indeed, as she finally realizes, she loves Rick beyond all scruple—unaware that Rick will settle for her admiration. The Rick-Annina analogy is more fitting as a portent of this climactic decision of Rick's, to send Ilsa away with Laszlo—for Rick, by fixing the roulette wheel, helps Annina get the visa money without capitulating to the *capitaine*.

Renault has his revenge when, at the suggestion of Major Strasser, he orders Rick's saloon closed. Earlier, Renault had told Rick that he allowed the place to stay open partly because Rick let him win at roulette. By assisting Annina, Rick made Renault lose. Now, Renault gestures dramatically toward the back room he has patronized for so long and says, "I'm shocked—*shocked* to find that there is gambling going on in here!" Thus, in one foul sweep, Renault satisfies Strasser with a genuine excuse for closing Rick's; indicates to Rick, through the absurdity of the charge, that it was Strasser's idea to close it, and not his; and pleases himself by taking revenge on Rick for depriving him of an evening's horizontal pleasure.

The café shut down, Ilsa returns for the letters of transit which she knows are in Rick's possession. Every ploy she tries—invoking the name of the Resistance, stirring the ashes of their Paris affair, calling him a coward, pleading with him, and finally threatening him—aggravates her barely suppressed hysterical love and increases his morose

196

fatalism. "Go ahead and shoot," Rick says. "You'll be doing me a favor." It is here that Ilsa realizes, not how much she overestimated his ability to withstand her departure in Paris, but how crushingly it affected his spirit. The man who, four years earlier, said of the Nazis, "I left a note in my apartment; they'll know where to find me," is now a handful of pulp waiting to be tossed away. Though Laszlo, the saint, has won her admiration, Rick's terse admission of his weakness, his humanity, wins her love. . . . How much I loved you, how much I still love you!"

But Rick has a ploy—noble, to be sure—of his own. Ilsa thinks she can stay with Rick and send Laszlo off to convert the masses, so Rick devises several artful decoys. *Someone,* he lets it be known, is going to use those letters of transit to leave Casablanca. Ilsa believes Laszlo will go alone; Renault believes Rick and Ilsa are going; and poor Laszlo believes he and Ilsa will be the lucky pair. Rick tells the truth only to the person he likes least; again, admiration is the operative motive. Rick contributes to The Cause by telling his rival the truth, and prolongs his mistress' love by lying to her. In both cases he is preserving illusions as well as saving lives—and, as regards Ilsa and Laszlo, preserving an illusion about Rick's "gesture" toward Ilsa may be the only way to save their life together.

Rick is as adept as Renault at the multiple ploy. It would appear he is about to make Strasser (and Renault) happy by promising to turn Laszlo over to them; make Ilsa happy by promising to leave with her; make Ferrari happy by selling the saloon—and Sam—to him. Actually, he is making himself happy by fooling all of them. Renault, ever the professional, tries to stop Rick from stepping into selflessness; but throughout the film, we have sensed indications that the Vichy-suave Captain, who shares with Rick a vaguely liberal wartime past, may be just corruptible enough to be bribed into political, if not stylistic, nobility. And so, when Rick dispatches Strasser and sends Ilsa and Laszlo off to the remote continent of North America, Renault orders his gendarme to "round up the usual suspects." True to form, Renault is incorrigibly corrupt: where he once evaded the law for sex, he now evades it for comradeship. As for Rick, his generosity masked the removal of an obsession whose poignancy had degenerated into the dull pain of an abscessed tooth. We have known all along that Rick's nobility consisted mainly in setting spilled glasses aright, asking Germans about the color of his eyes, and squeezing a profit out of a café whose specialties were Molotov cocktails of political intrigue. Renault's order to his gendarme is the password into Rick's exclusive new club: The Order of the Heroic Pragmatist. What better place than the edge of the Sahara, and what better companion than Renault, for "the beginning of a beautiful friendship"?

IV

Like the very best Hollywood films (*Citizen Kane, The Searchers, Psycho*), but unlike works by the European commercial avant-garde, *Casablanca* succeeds as allegory, popular myth, clinical psychology or whatever, *and* as a superb romantic melodrama. The writers and Curtiz don't ruin their epiphanies with overexplicit dialogue or long pauses that give us time to consider double and triple meanings. Superficially, *Casablanca* is another Bogart vehicle, driven at Warners' usual reckless pace, and shifting emotional gears at the climax so we can be sure enough of Bogey's soft-hearted tough-guy to return in a few months for his next picture. Rich as it is—though not terrifyingly deep—the film is so damned entertaining that we don't need the spur of a doctoral thesis or cultural insecurity to prod us to see it again and again. And the script that Koch hastily wrote on the substructure of the earlier Epstein efforts—a job that virtually defines Grace Under Pressure (Hollywood-style)—reads so beautifully that, with its publication, many Casablancaphiles may swear off the torture-seats of the local repertory cinema or the commercial interruptions of TV revivals for a shorter, but no less rewarding, pilgrimage to their nearest bookshelf.

198

Howard Barnes
Bosley Crowther

ORIGINAL REVIEWS

⌐ON THE SCREEN⌐

By HOWARD BARNES

"Casablanca"—Hollywood

"CASABLANCA." a screenplay by Julius J. and Philip
G. Epstein and Howard Koch, from a play by Murray
Burnett and Joan Alison, directed by Michael Curtiz,
produced by Hal B. Wallis, presented by Warner Bros.
Pictures at the Hollywood Theater with the following cast:

Rick	Humphrey Bogart
Ilsa Lund	Ingrid Bergman
Victor Laszlo	Paul Henreid
Captain Louis Renault	Claude Rains
Major Strasser	Conrad Veidt
Senor Ferrari	Sidney Greenstreet
Ugarte	Peter Lorre
Carl, a waiter	S. Z. Sakall
Yvonne	Madeleine Le Beau
Sam	Dooley Wilson
Annina Brandel	Joy Page
Berger	John Qualen
Sascha, a bartender	Leonid Kinskey
Jan	Helmut Dantine
Dark European	Curt Bois
Croupier	Marcel Dalio
Singer	Corinna Mura
Mr. Leuchtag	Ludwig Stossel
Mrs. Leuchtag	Ilka Gruning
Senor Martinez	Charles La Torre
Arab Vendor	Frank Puglia
Abdul	Dan Seymour

The kaleidoscopic events of recent weeks have made
"Casablanca" impressively topical. The new picture at the

Hollywood Theater keys into the headlines with prophetic insight. It exposes the intrigue, political shilly-shally and anti-Fascist resentment which must have been the background for the present Allied offensive in Northwest Africa. At the same time, it is a smashing and moving melodrama in its own right. Good writing, a brilliant cast and artful direction add up here to a superior show, as well as a significant document.

The casting of this Warner Bros. production has been prodigal. Humphrey Bogart and Sidney Greenstreet, who were so good in "The Maltese Falcon" and "Across the Pacific," are once more on hand to give the production ominous and violent potentialities. Meanwhile, there is Ingrid Bergman, playing the heroine of a war picture with all her appealing authority and beauty. And the lesser parts are filled by such knowing performers as Paul Henreid, Conrad Veidt, Claude Rains, Peter Lorre, John Qualen and S. Z. Sakall.

With such a company, a dull script might have made the grade. The fact is that "Casablanca" has a continuity which is a clever blend of melodrama and meaning. There are preposterous moments in the proceedings, as when an embittered American bistro proprietor in Casablanca permits a leader of the European underground movement to escape with the woman he loves; but the show makes a great deal of sense, in addition to being a striking thriller. It has sustained interest as well as excitement. Put it on your recommended list of current screen entertainments.

Bogart is an old hand at this sort of muted melodrama. He has rarely been more forceful than he is as a disillusioned democrat, fighting the Axis long before the rest of his compatriots. Miss Bergman illuminates every scene in which she appears in the role of a Norwegian beauty who falls in love with an American soldier of fortune, but leaves her erstwhile lover to continue the good fight against Nazi aggression. Henreid, Rains, Lorre, Veidt and the others contribute incisive portraits of the curious human tapestry of a desert city which has sprung into prominence long after the film was made.

Michael Curtiz has not let his players down. He has staged "Casablanca" with power and imagination. There is a memorable scene in which a Gestapo gang starts singing German songs in the saloon of the American soldier of fortune and are drowned out by the "Marseillaise." There are sequences of oblique suspense which add tremendously to the total effect of the melodrama. "Casablanca" happens to be timely. It also happens to be an excellent film.

'Casablanca,' With Humphrey Bogart and Ingrid Bergman, at Hollywood— 'White Cargo' and 'Ravaged Earth' Open

CASABLANCA; screenplay by Julius J. and Philip G. Epstein and Howard Koch; from a play by Murray Burnett and Joan Alison; directed by Michael Curtiz; produced by Hal B. Wallis for Warner Brothers. At the Hollywood.

By BOSLEY CROWTHER

Against the electric background of a sleek café in a North African port, through which swirls a backwash of connivers, crooks and fleeing European refugees, the Warner Brothers are telling a rich, suave, exciting and moving tale in their new film, "Casablanca," which came to the Hollywood yesterday. They are telling it in the high tradition of their hard-boiled romantic-adventure style. And to make it all the more tempting they have given it a top-notch thriller cast of Humphrey Bogart, Sidney Greenstreet, Peter Lorre, Conrad Veidt and even Claude Rains, and have capped it magnificently with Ingrid Bergman, Paul Henreid and a Negro "find" named Dooley Wilson.

Yes, indeed, the Warners here have a picture which makes the spine tingle and the heart take a leap. For once more, as in recent Bogart pictures, they have turned the incisive trick of draping a tender love story within the folds of a tight topical theme. They have used Mr. Bogart's

203

personality, so well established in other brilliant films, to inject a cold point of tough resistance to evil forces afoot in Europe today. And they have so combined sentiment, humor and pathos with taut melodrama and bristling intrigue that the result is a highly entertaining and even inspiring film.

The story, as would be natural, has its devious convolutions of plot. But mainly it tells of a tough fellow named Rick who runs a Casablanca café and of what happens (or what happened last December) when there shows up in his joint one night a girl whom he had previously loved in Paris in company with a fugitive Czech patriot. The Nazis are tailing the young Czech; the Vichy officials offer only brief refuge—and Rick holds the only two sure passports which will guarantee his and the girl's escape. But Rick loves the girl very dearly, she is now married to this other man—and whenever his Negro pianist sits there in the dark and sings "As Time Goes By" that old, irresistible feeling consumes him in a choking, maddening wave.

Don't worry; we won't tell you how it all comes out. That would be rankest sabotage. But we will tell you that the urbane detail and the crackling dialogue which has been packed into this film by the scriptwriters, the Epstein brothers and Howard Koch, is of the best. We will tell you that Michael Curtiz has directed for slow suspense and that his camera is always conveying grim tension and uncertainty. Some of the significant incidents, too, are affecting— such as that in which the passionate Czech patriot rouses the customers in Rick's cafe to drown out a chorus of Nazis by singing the "Marseillaise," or any moment in which Dooley Wilson is remembering past popular songs in a hushed room.

We will tell you also that the performances of the actors are all of the first order, but especially those of Mr. Bogart and Miss Bergman in the leading roles. Mr. Bogart is, as usual, the cool, cynical, efficient and super-wise guy as becomes his inner character, and he handles it credibly. Miss Bergman is surpassingly lovely, crisp and natural as the girl and lights the romantic passages with a warm and genuine glow.

Mr. Rains is properly slippery and crafty as a minion

of Vichy perfidy, and Mr. Veidt plays again a Nazi officer with cold and implacable resolve. Very little is demanded of Mr. Greenstreet as a shrewd black-market trader, but that is good, and Mr. Henreid is forthright and simple as the imperiled Czech patriot. Mr. Wilson's performance as Rick's devoted friend, though rather brief, is filled with a sweetness and compassion which lend a helpful mood to the whole film, and other small roles are played ably by S. Z. Sakall, Joy Page, Leonid Kinskey and Mr. Lorre.

In short, we will say that "Casablanca" is one of the year's most exciting and trenchant films. It certainly won't make Vichy happy—but that's just another point for it.

(*Note:* The italicized selections in the following are quotes from the interviews of members of the Stanford community by Walter Bougere, a recent graduate and a Fellini scholar. Since successive generations of young people, including the present one, have adopted *Casablanca* as their own, it seems appropriate to include a number of their comments, which appear fairly typical of their age group and which give some indication of the personal and social context in which the film is viewed. While not necessarily proving anything, they happen to parallel some of my own observations on motion pictures, past and present, included in this chapter.)

Howard Koch

IN CONCLUSION: WHAT HAPPENED TO STORY IN THE CONTEMPORARY FILM?

It is no secret that motion picture production in the seventies is in serious trouble. Hollywood as we knew it in the days of *Casablanca* no longer exists. Aside from a few used for television production, the huge, cavernous stages on the studio lots are ghostly vestiges of past glory. Films are now made all over the world, mostly by independents, and are financed by sources as diverse as industrial conglomerates and American Indian tribes. Recalling some of the well-publicized sins of Hollywood's so-called factory production, we might assume this to be a favorable development for the motion picture from both a commercial and an artistic standpoint. However, it is at least questionable whether this assumption has been borne out in either case.

According to *Variety* figures, the majority of films made today are box-office failures. There are notable exceptions, of course: the golden half-dozen or so each year that practically monopolize the circuits and return vast sums of money to their investors. Some not on this favored list are able to recoup their losses, or even make a profit, from the addition of record and television sales.

Granted that it is unrealistic to draw an equation between popular success and a film's real worth, since people go to movies for all sorts of reasons, I would never dismiss audience response to the emotional content of a picture as a fairly accurate gauge of its validity. In my experience as a screenwriter I found an audience's reaction to a film far more sensitive than the condescending assessment I used to hear so often in Hollywood story conferences.

While there is apparently a diminishing audience for contemporary films, movies produced several decades ago like *Treasure of the Sierra Madre, Citizen Kane, High Noon,* and *Casablanca,* to name only a few of the better-known, continue to draw large audiences both to the television screen and to their revivals at the neighborhood

208

theatres. In a recent program of twenty "classics" announced by the Elgin Cinema and fairly typical of such lists, fifteen were made during the thirties and forties, only five in the fifties and sixties.

To me this raised an interesting question. Will the motion pictures produced in recent times be shown over and over again thirty years from now? Some will, of course. Certain films directed by Fellini, Truffaut, Antonioni, and Bergman have already acquired a revival status that is likely to endure. Others such as *The Battle of Algiers, The Organizer,* and *The Conformist* might very well appear in the lists of future "classics." However, judging from the limited response of today's audiences to most films made in this period, the number will be both fewer and more specialized in their appeal than the films made in the "Hollywood" era. Since young people provide a large proportion of the movie-going public, some typical comments of the Stanford students interviewed might be pertinent.

"There was a strength and optimism, a wonderful spirit in the 30's and 40's films. It was a great era of film-making. In modern movies people seem like models; there's no relationship. They just pass in front of you in this shiny gloss like flickering symbols, but you can't get into them."
> Robin Menken McDonald, 24,
> improvisational actress.
> She has seen *Casablanca* 4 times.

"I just love the movie so much. I go to see it about once a year. Those clever dialogue movies aren't made any more where it's interesting just to hear people talk. I sit there and mumble the lines. I practically know them all by heart."
> Ellen Lewin, 25, anthropologist.
> She has seen *Casablanca* 11 times.

"My first response to it is like greeting an old friend. My mother always forgets how good it is

until I make her watch it on the late show. She never sees the point to start watching it and then she can't leave it."

Leonard Schwarz, 27, a writer.
He has seen *Casablanca* 6 times.

This is not to suggest that we go back to making movies as we made them in the Hollywood era. During the intervening years the film has advanced immeasurably both in technique and in sophistication. Liberated from censorship and freed from the physical confinement of the stages, we can attempt any subject and shoot it in its natural location. Technically, the improvements are enormous. Cameras, raw stock, and sound equipment are so refined as to make those used in the thirties and forties seem primitive. In what area then is the average contemporary film less satisfying to the general run of audiences than its predecessors?

In my opinion it is their increasing emphasis on effect at the expense of content, the *mise-en-scène* taking precedence over a structured story. By story in a film sense I mean a narrative with a logical flow of incidents involving characters with whose emotions and motivations audiences can identify because they reflect some aspect of universal experience.

Very often we hear today's movie-goers—and I'm one of them—say as they come away from the theatre, "That scene in the car [*Five Easy Pieces*] was hilarious" or "That photography [*Downhill Racer*] was superb. How did they ever get those shots?" etc. Only rarely are we so moved by a film that we are reluctant to discuss it in intellectual or piecemeal terms because we have shared in a satisfying emotional experience. Many recent movies can impress us with their photographic beauty, titillate us with their sexuality, and give us sadistic thrills with their literal depiction of brutality, but only occasionally do they enlist our feelings. The desire for emotional involvement came up repeatedly in the comments of the young people in the Stanford community.

210

"It's really nice to go to a film with your girl friend and know that you're both there for the emotional experience and you both accept that in each other and you can have it together. Especially for me because I've always played a role, learning to be a man and not showing my emotions. Casablanca *is a way to get out of that kind of thing. We were allowing each other to be young in each other's presence, being able to cry and get excited about a movie. You know, certain parts I was saying, 'Oh, wow. Isn't that cool. Out of sight. Far-out script.' Being really excited instead of saying 'Hum, interesting movie,' in an intellectual way."*

Lew Andrews, 24, student.
He has seen *Casablanca* 13 times.

"When Captain Renault, after that long pause, tells his troops to round up the usual supects, it was impossible to keep back a wild applause. It was just engulfing. There was ecstatic joy. The whole theatre at that point went up in a large cheer. It was a kind of universal thing."

Jack Kenealy, 18, student.
He has seen the film twice.

"The characters said something about life. Sometimes you lose track of the Rick in yourself and in other people, or the Laszlo in yourself, or the Sam and Ilsa in yourself. It's nice to see it all come together."

Dilip Mirchandani, 21, student from India. He has seen *Casablanca* twice.

"When I see a movie and it really touches me or I really get involved in it, I carry the feeling away with me from the theatre. I can go on for days feeling the sort of way Casablanca *made me feel."*

Caprice Schmidt, 16, a potter.
Saw the film recently for the first time.

211

In so many areas of modern living we have become spectators, whether it's a political event we're watching or a football game or a movie. In neither the real world nor the fictional world are we asked to participate. The images flash across our screens and we look at them from an emotional distance. The eye is sated while the heart is left hungry.

Instead of an organic whole, "beautiful in the sense that it is an ordered film, well worked out" as one Stanford student put it, the average contemporary movie is more likely to be a succession of illustrative scenes, often effective in themselves, that seem to have been pasted together in the cutting rooms.

This impression is reinforced by statements made by various directors themselves. In an article in *The New York Times* magazine section, Robert Altman, the director of *M*A*S*H,* claims that he together with his actors "make" a film on the set "like an artist painting a picture . . . a good movie is taking the narrative out, taking the story out of it" and the *Times* reporter added: "Throughout the picture it was rare for Altman to know one morning exactly what he was going to be filming the next morning." The work of the original author, Richard Hooker, and that of the screenwriter, Ring Lardner, Jr., are cast aside as disposable waste products of the director's creative effort.

Another exponent of improvisation on the set is John Cassavetes. In his film, *Husbands,* we spend most of the first hour in a bar watching his three male characters poking and slapping each other while making adolescent sounds that pass for dialogue. The intent, no doubt, was to be "spontaneous" and "natural" but I don't believe people go to a movie for a literal depiction of what they see all too often in their everyday lives. At least, the audience with whom I saw the picture was visibly bored—and boring an audience seems to me a cardinal sin even if the film-maker's purpose is to portray the shallowness and boredom of his characters. If this is the way Cassavetes believes errant husbands behave after the death of a friend, he might have spared us some of the length and given us more depth. But this would have required an exercise of craftsmanship and an imaginative probing into the

212

nuances of behavior that no director, however talented, can be expected to generate extemporaneously on a movie set.

An extreme practitioner of making a movie without a script, and without even a story except as it emerges during the shooting, is Norman Mailer. While I have great admiration for Mailer as a novelist, a reporter, and a catalyst, I consider his "course in film-making" expounded in an article in the *New American Review 12* as a spurious rationalization by an amateur who tries to make films on the strength of his literary reputation without submitting himself to the disciplines of creating a dramatic work. Admitting he has skipped over any movie-making apprenticeship, Mailer claims he has found a "novel technique . . . closer to the nature of film than the work of other, more talented directors." It seems to me not unlike a musician claiming he is a better composer because he never bothered to learn the scale.

In the article he described how the Mailer-made technique worked in practice during the shooting of *Maidstone*. Assembling a number of his friends along with a professional leading man, Rip Torn, on an estate, he "waited for things to happen" so that he could photograph them as they occurred. Well, apparently things did eventually happen— "balling in midnight beds and pools," alcoholic encounters, and accidents leading up to the big event, a fight between the director and the leading man during which Mailer got hit over the head with a hammer by Rip Torn and Torn got his ear chewed by Mailer. It was this climactic incident which, according to Mailer, provided him with "an entire new conception of the movie." I suppose if one is willing to lose a little blood, this orgiastic method is at least easier than working for four months on a screenplay.

In my view Mailer was not creating a dramatic work at all; he was reporting a "happening" on film, but the event he was recording was not a genuine one, either present or historical, that might be the subject of a documentary. Instead, he was photographing a series of synthetic incidents brewed out of alcohol, sex, and frayed tempers. What emerged from this cinema un-vérité was a glorified home movie which I doubt would ever have been

213

shown outside his circle of friends had Mailer's name not been attached.

As a writer I am naturally not enamored with the whole *auteur* approach to film-making and, as a movie fan, I find the director's improvisational style no adequate substitute for a well-told story. From time immemorial stories and legends have been passed down from generation to generation as a collective heritage of our race. Whether oral or written, those that live on in our memories and our literature do so because they reveal some aspect of truth identifiable with our experience. We do not ask them to be factually true—that is for the reporters and historians. Yet many film-makers today apparently regard story as "out of style," claiming by one method or another to give us a more literal truth. But no matter how hard they try to generate life spontanenously on the screen, they can never succeed. The players on the stage and their shadows on the screen are miming life, not living it. Hopefully, if the dramatist or screenwriter has provided them with the essentials, they are contributing to a work of art.

In films it is the screenplay that is supposed to contain those essential elements that make up a story. Some years ago I wrote an article for *Sight and Sound,* an English magazine of film criticism, in which I took exception to the theory of one of its director-contributors that the function of the screenwriter should be limited to furnishing lines of dialogue for insertion in the visual pattern created by the director. My article raised such a storm you would think I'd attacked the Magna Carta. The magazine devoted most of its next issue to various counterattacks, which somehow I survived, unrepentant and unconvinced.

It was and still is my contention that one cannot arbitrarily separate the visual ideas from the auditory and that both together, comprising the content of the film, must pre-exist as an entity in someone's imagination. This basic creative task, I maintain, is properly the writer's and not the director's, however much he may add to, or subtract from, the continuity as set down in the screenplay. I realize that a director may also happen to be a dramatist and be the sole or a participating author of the script, as is often the case today, but the fact that one man may assume a dual function is beside the point. Nor does it necessarily prove that he is qualified simply because he is in a position of power that enables him to assume a writer's prerogative. Needless to say, my article didn't convert *Sight and Sound* nor any of the European critics, who still speak of films as though they were immaculately conceived by the director and delivered on the set in a last-minute spasm of improvisation.

The writing of *Casablanca,* recounted in an earlier chapter, might appear to support the opposing view but, even under the pressure of meeting deadlines, the film was not "improvised" in the usual sense. The time spent by the Epsteins and myself in developing the story and screenplay before and during production amounted to at least three months. Nor was it written by the director and actors on the set, although they made valuable contributions. Even so, the conditions under which the film was made would usually spell disaster, but *Casablanca* seemed to have a charmed life.

Even under ideal circumstances the construction of any dramatic work is an extremely demanding process which, throughout history, has required the private hours of a disciplined mind committing its thoughts to paper. In building a scene the dramatist must pre-visualize the action and reaction of every participating character, he must pre-audit every line of dialogue, he must anticipate every emotion and relate every idea to the work as a whole. I can't imagine why this complex creativity, when applied to films, can best be carried on while the actors are waiting on the set and the camera is breathing down the creator's neck. A well-written scene isn't like fish—it doesn't spoil with age. Properly directed and acted, it will seem to be spontaneous even though it may have been written a month ago, a year ago, or a thousand years ago. The spontaneity on the screen for which there is presently a passion is not necessarily achieved by improvisation on the set. I doubt if Beethoven conceived many of his symphonic ideas while the orchestra was tuning up.

Until very recently the screenplay was considered a bastard form with no literary identity of its own and was

215

mostly hidden from public view. But lately a number of publishers have recognized its existence and have discovered, among film-oriented readers, a latent demand for its appearance in a published version. However, in most movie reviews the screenplay is still treated as a subordinate element in the director's creation.

Some time ago I raised this question of film authorship with one of the New York newspaper critics, a conscientious and thoughtful man, who gave me a sensible answer. "How do we know who did what? We don't see the script before its screening, we don't know what the writer contributed. The film is shown to us as the director's and that's the way we have to accept and appraise it." Undoubtedly this is true but I pointed out that the theatre critic in the adjacent column reviews the stage play as primarily the work of the playwright who wrote it while the director's contribution is assessed in terms of the staging and interpretation.

Why this basic distinction? Anyone who has read a professionally written screenplay is aware that its content is much the same as for a stage play except with less dialogue and more description of visualized movement because of the nature of the film medium. Unlike other literary forms, neither a play nor a film script can be regarded as a really complete work until the written words are translated into the speech and behavior of actors playing before an audience—in the one case on a stage, in the other photographed and shown on a screen. No one has satisfactorily explained why this mechanical distinction accounts for the assumption that a dramatist writing for the stage is considered the original source of the content while, in writing for films, he is merely an appendage to the director, who by some strange alchemy becomes the author.

The reasons, I believe, are in large part historical. In the more primitive era of silent pictures, there was no need for a screenplay. The director was in complete control of the making of a film. If he needed a writer at all, it was to prepare a "scenario," which was a loose outline of the general movement of the story and which usually could be concocted by any bright ten-year-old

216

child. It is significant that the term "scenario" and "scenarist" are carried over into the vocabulary of many European directors and critics today—words that no longer have any relevance to what the writer contributes to the modern sound film. Another vestige from the past is the term "script-writer," which always conjures up to me the image of a monk in some monastery cell copying scripture on parchment with a quill.

As the movie-making system evolved, the star became the negotiable factor in the so-called "package," which pretty much determined what films could be made. And the director was usually the key to the star's approval of a project. There were perhaps twenty or thirty directors in the world who could command the relatively few stars in each country whose box-office potential assured the financing of a production. There wasn't a single writer who could do the same, no matter how well known or successful he may have been as a dramatist in films or in the theatre. The star was, of course, vitally interested in the screenplay since it contained the elements out of which he must build his characterization, but it was the director to whom he looked for his security. His was the visible presence on the set. It was his reassuring voice that said "Fine, print that" at the end of a take. If the director happened to be "hot," meaning exuding heat from a recent success, he could often obtain a star's consent to appear in a picture before reading the screenplay or even before it was written. Moreover, the director was part of the establishment, he had ready access to the studio heads, who looked to him to bring in a marketable picture on the allotted budget. Writers, on the other hand, were regarded as a breed apart and somewhat suspect.

As the major studios with their stables of contract players disintegrated, the director's power increased to the point where at the present time he, rather than the star, has become the key figure in putting together a production. While there are still four or five actors or actresses whose names automatically guarantee a large audience, the star system has, in the main, been replaced by the director in his new role as *auteur*. The public may not know his name but those who finance and distribute film are fully

217

aware of his standing and his record, and would then, on this basis, determine what pictures will be made.

It is not my intention to minimize the importance of the film director nor to maintain that his function isn't creative as well as interpretive. Having been luckier than many screenwriters in working with directors of the caliber of Max Ophuls, William Wyler, Orson Welles, John Huston, Howard Hawks, and Michael Curtiz, I have the greatest respect for their accomplishments. I am also aware that the writing of a screenplay is only the first step in a long process.

While I believe the screenplay should establish the basic content—the theme, the story continuity, and the characterizations—the director must be free to use his own creative resources in translating words on paper to their fullest visual expression on the screen. In my opinion there is no "author" of a film in the same sense as there is an author of a novel or short story. While the director is and should be the dominant figure during the shooting, it seems obvious that a motion picture, by the nature of its multiple facets, is a collective work. Writer and director, when not the same person, are interdependent not only on each other but on all the contributing artists and craftsmen from the actors and cameraman to the music composer.

Taking an opposing view is the statement of a talented American director, Elia Kazan, as quoted in a *New York Times* interview: "Any picture to be any good at all must be made by the director. . . . The director has to make that choice of continuity of images that is the motion picture. . . . This continuity is the director's job." Mr. Kazan has worked with writers of the caliber of Arthur Miller and Tennessee Williams. Does he really mean to say that *Death of a Salesman* and *A Streetcar Named Desire* are, in any exclusive sense, his pictures? No doubt he contributed to both the stage and screen versions of these two works, but the continuity of action on the stage and the continuity of images on the screen were not primarily his. The statement he made demonstrates how pervasive is the fiction that a director "makes" a film, despite the most obvious evidence that its basic content was the creative work of an established dramatist.

218

The *auteur* theory was first popularized by *Cahiers du Cinema* and the New Wave, which made its influence felt in this country with the arrival of films by Truffaut, Godard, and other distinguished French directors. In its inception, the New Wave made an important contribution to the development and maturity of the motion picture. In Hollywood we had, in a sense, learned our craft too well— excessive virtue can sometimes be a vice. Many of our films were so neatly constructed that you could see the plot wheels turning and anticipate their movement. The unexpected, the perverse is in the nature of life but was too seldom reflected on our screen. New Wave films like *The 400 Blows* relaxed our tight story construction without sacrificing its inner logic.

However, in the course of time this desirable flexibility and freedom initiated by these film-makers turned into a self-indulgent use of the medium for a more or less exclusive coterie of critics and aestheticians. In an interview in *Film Comment* Truffaut laid bare this attitude:

"Now that I make films and the question of quality of the film hardly interests me anymore, this is what I look for. I try to spot whether the man who made it was violent, calm, happy, angry—and I look at it scene by scene and this way I try to get back to the source, to the character, the personality of the director. I can almost sense whether in such and such a scene the director was happy with his actors or was angry at what they were doing. I now look at films almost in the way one would examine a temperature chart at the foot of a hospital bed. . . . There are not good and bad films—there are simply good and bad directors. . . . You might have a situation where a good director makes a 'bad' picture but, nevertheless, this film would have more interest for the critic than the 'good' film by the bad director."

> *"I no longer enjoy the foreign art films as much as I used to. The thing I like most now is the thing I was most snobbish about before, really good entertainment."*

Stephen Stept, 24, student.
He has seen *Casablanca* twice.

Possibly M. Truffaut didn't realize that he and his New Wave colleagues were opening the flood gates to the egocentricities of less talented directors. Nor does this attitude show any consideration for the audience who pays an admission to see the film. It seems unlikely that the average movie-goer has the slightest interest in the emotional state of the director. More recently *Cahiers du Cinema,* perhaps after taking a hard look at the financial plight of the French film industry, has begun to promote what they term "structuralism," which I assume refers to a more structured film than the kind they espoused in the past. Andrew Sarris, critic, has this to say in the *Village Voice* of July 9, 1970, "But it strikes me suddenly that the transition of *Cahiers* from the Politique des Auteurs to Structuralism is not without a certain logic. . . . Nowadays when every hack goes to outlandish lengths to make a personal statement, the sobering discipline of structuralism as a critical policy may be a useful device to limit artistic presumption."

My own movie-going confirms this belated recognition that a reassessment of the *auteur*-made film is overdue. Recently I saw a picture so bad it shall be nameless. Its young American director, apparently determined to outdo his predecessors, gave such an exhibition of stylistic gymnastics as to baffle the mind and strain the eyesight. He shot in fast motion, slow motion, and no motion. He jump-cut with such delirious abandon I never knew where I was—in the present, the past, or the future. His leading actor, a singularly unattractive young man, was scrutinized by the camera in every position, even upside down, and at times so closely that his facial pores stood out like craters on the moon. When he kissed his girl friend, his lips were so enlarged, like the mouth of some giant blow-fish, I was afraid he was going to swallow her. I sat there fascinated for ninety minutes wondering whether the story—if that's the word for it—might finally make a little sense. It never did.

Admittedly, this is an extravagant example of a director's "authorship." But it brings into clear focus the salient question that affects all of us—movie-maker and movie-goer alike. Should the content of a film determine its style or should style be an end in itself? Or to put it

220

another way, are we to use the screen to tell a story or as a showcase for the director's personal expression? Judging from the plight of the movie industry today, the *auteur* vogue is not succeeding in purely commerical terms. A prominent English film executive recently stated his view in the *Times:* "We have to stop making pictures for directors and go back to making them for audiences."

But what about the artistic pretensions of the *auteur* film? Have we gained in art what we lost in commerce? I suppose that depends on one's definition of art. To some the more obscure the film's meaning, the more subjective its content, the less it communicates with its audience, the higher its artistic quotient. If it is chaotic in its stylistic expression and dehumanized in its character delineation, well, isn't the contemporary world chaotic and dehumanized? Shouldn't a film reflect the era in which it is made? Obviously there are many film-makers and critics today who hold this view.

However, there is another definition of art which I prefer, one formulated by Havelock Ellis many years ago: "Art is the recreation of the world after the heart's desire." Granted that all values are in flux and that 20th-century man is in moral confusion, isn't it the proper function of the artist, in whatever medium he works, to attempt to bring some order out of chaos instead of merely reflecting or compounding the confusion? After the intellectualizing of their elders failed to provide a way of life they can respect, the young people of today are obviously searching for a new set of values nearer to their "heart's desire."

> *"Films like that* (Casablanca) *show you things you really long for. There are all those graspable values floating around in the film. It's full of a lost heritage that we can't live. Life is no longer like that. The most moving part of the film is the Marseillaise scene. Everyone stands together. A tremendous sense of patriotism. Maybe it's an emotion we're starved for, a luxury other generations have been able to afford but we have to go without. A nice dream."*
>
> Jon Else, 26, a film-maker.
> He has seen *Casablanca* twice.

221

"In this country, it is a fact of life, I think, that most radicals want to be loved. Casablanca *is the kind of film that makes a radical feel he's part of the mainstream."*

Jim Bransten, 26, political activist.
He has seen *Casablanca* 3 times.

"In some ways it gets you in spite of yourself, like in the super-patriotic things, the scene with the Marseillaise and all that. It gets the old blood to stirring even if you're not basically inclined that way. I don't think my reaction was really a matter of patriotism. It was a matter of the good guys against the bad guys. So it was getting you on the idealistic side, hitting there. I felt exhilarated. I was sort of bouncing up and down. When I think of it, I feel warm, like when I think about a good friend of mine.

Coralia Serafim, 27, reference
librarian at Stanford. She
recently saw *Casablanca* for the
first time.

———

In the interests of presenting a balanced summary, the following quotes reveal that, even among *Casablanca's* youthful fans, there were occasional reservations. Both of these negative reactions centered on the "Marseillaise" scene. Allowing for the vastly different character of World War II (the period of the film) and Vietnam and the greater awareness today of colonialism, I still feel that the objections expressed by these two young men have enough validity and pertinence to merit their inclusion.

"The thing that bothered me most in the whole film was that I felt a real surge of fervor when they started singing 'The Marseillaise.' I really wanted to stand up with all of them. The film was effective in grabbing that feeling. At the same time I knew it was that very feeling that produced the war in the first place. It was enough people standing up and singing their national anthem with enough fervor. Those

feelings need to be fulfilled but I know that their way of fulfilling them is a lie and I've got to find my own way. It would be nice if I could stand up with them and sing with them but I can't because I know what they're singing is out of key with what I hear. The need is to have something outside of ourselves that we believe in, that we're willing to come together for and share that sense of brotherhood. And I guess that is what feeds into the counter-culture. The feeling is there that we're working toward something that we mutually believe in and that we can work together for. Even though we don't know where we're going, we know the direction is good."

Myrl Manley, 24, nursery school
teacher. He has seen *Casablanca* once.

"It's never mentioned in the film that neither the Germans nor the French have any business having their armies in Morocco. The French are as culpable for ruling Casablanca as the Germans are for ruling Paris, yet nowhere in the film is there a hint of this contradiction. Apart from being corrupt, Captain Renault's power in Casablanca is not shown as socially unjust. Ostensibly those singing the 'Marseillaise' are making a gesture against tyranny but it is hard to imagine the singing of a patriotic Moroccan song bringing the same reaction."

Walter Bougere, Stanford graduate.
He has seen *Casablanca* 7 times.

Like pilgrims, they go back time and again to a film made thirty years ago, a simple melodrama, to find an emotional release and to renew their hope for a more humanistic society of the future. Perhaps they are telling us something important that is missing today both in our lives and in our films.

223